Tiana

Thought you ar[b]...
enjoy this hidden...

Sharon

MW01067998

PRAISE FOR

ALL THE KING'S HORSES

"A wonderful account of how Elvis Presley, living under the mega wattage of his super stardom, found his ultimate solace and deepest center in the company of his horses. A testament to the healing power of these majestic, noble animals. His relationship with Rising Sun, his beloved Palomino, reads like a love affair. A marvelous book!"

> —**CHRISTINE BARANSKI**, multiple Tony and Emmy Award winning actress, and star of the CBS All Access series, *The Good Fight*

"After reading *All the King's Horses*, I could almost imagine standing next to Elvis and gazing into his horse's eyes. This well-written book takes you into a little known world where Elvis felt the most at ease; with his equine friends. You can feel Elvis's devotion to his horses. Elvis and horses. What could be any better?"

> —**JEANNE MARIE MIRABITO**, founder and president, Our Mims Retirement Haven, Paris, KY

"Just when you thought you knew everything about Elvis, Victoria Racimo and Kim Gatto unveil one of the most important relationships of his life. Surrounded by hangers-on and sycophants along with adoring fans, Elvis longed for a few minutes of quiet…with a creature who didn't want anything but love. None of the hundreds of biographies came close to discovering how much his equine friends meant to the King. Until now."

> —**MICHAEL BLOWEN**, founder and president, Old Friends, Georgetown, KY

"This meticulously researched book is a must read for people who love horses and love Elvis. Riding was clearly a way for The King to get away from the pressures of fame and *All the King's Horses* shows a little-known side of Elvis and how his love for his horses grounded and energized his life."

> —**JANE GOLDENRING**, film and television producer, President of Goldenring Productions, and former Sr. VP of Production at Disney

"In their fascinating and revealing new book *All the King's Horses: The Equestrian Life of Elvis Presley*, Victoria Racimo and Kimberly Gatto begin with the old adage, 'There is something about the outside of a horse that is good for the inside of a man.' No quote is more appropriate in describing the profound, almost spiritual effect horses had on a man who was worshiped by millions of adoring fans all over the world who only knew the outside of Elvis Presley. In this beautifully told and meticulously researched adventure of discovery, Racimo and Gatto dig deep into that side of Elvis no one ever saw and show you the inside of a man."

> —**STEVE HASKIN**, award-winning Hall of Fame American horse racing journalist and author

"Elvis's love of horses is palpable in this wonderful new book. They touched his soul and became his passion! He finally found peace and solace when he was around them, often riding alone for hours, giving him a much-needed escape. I loved learning about this soft and gentle side of the King. A really fun and fast read. Great job, Victoria and Kimberly. Thanks for giving us this story. A must read for Elvis fans!"

> —**ROBIN HUTTON**, author of the *New York Times* bestseller, *Sgt. Reckless: America's War Horse*

"What always interests me is highlighted by this book: human relationships/friendships with animals. The need for animals in our lives is the need for a re-democratization of us as fellow sufferers and fellow travellers through creation. Loss of that democracy is also paradoxically a loss of humanity. With a celebrity like Elvis, the need to rediscover or reboot his humility must have been both powerful and unattainable with other human beings. He was just too big. The story of Elvis seeking his democracy among his equine friends is very [heart]warming in Racimo and Gatto's book, *All the King's Horses*."

> —**BERNARD POMERANCE**, author and Tony Award-winning playwright of *The Elephant Man*

"Reading about the comforting relationships Elvis had with his horses, I learned there was a very different side to the superstar. How lovely to know that Elvis the man, the husband, the father, the friend—found a special place to go with his equine friends when everything else was in the crazy zone. This book gave me insight into his overwhelming kindness, generosity, and spirit."

> —**SHARON A. CARR**, Broadway producer, *Pippin*, *Trip to Bountiful*, *Cinderella*

"If you love Elvis, if you love horses, (and I do love Elvis and I do love horses), then you won't be able to put down *All the King's Horses*. I finally found something that Elvis and I have in common!"

> —**MIKEY CAMERON**, ESPN Radio Lex talk show host, and thoroughbred racehorse trainer/breeder

All the King's Horses

ALL THE KING'S HORSES

The Equestrian Life of ELVIS PRESLEY

KIMBERLY GATTO and VICTORIA RACIMO
Foreword by Elvis confidant **LARRY GELLER**

REGNERY
HISTORY

Copyright © 2017 by Victoria Racimo and Kimberly Gatto

All rights reserved. No part of this publication may be reproduced or transmitted in any form or by any means electronic or mechanical, including photocopy, recording, or any information storage and retrieval system now known or to be invented, without permission in writing from the publisher, except by a reviewer who wishes to quote brief passages in connection with a review written for inclusion in a magazine, newspaper, website, or broadcast.

Regnery History™ is a trademark of Salem Communications Holding Corporation
Regnery® is a registered trademark of Salem Communications Holding Corporation

Cataloging-in-Publication data on file with the Library of Congress

ISBN 978-1-62157-603-7

Published in the United States by
Regnery History
An imprint of Regnery Publishing
A Division of Salem Media Group
300 New Jersey Ave NW
Washington, DC 20001
www.RegneryHistory.com

Manufactured in the United States of America

10 9 8 7 6 5 4 3 2 1

Books are available in quantity for promotional or premium use. For information on discounts and terms, please visit our website: www.Regnery.com.

Distributed to the trade by
Perseus Distribution
www.perseusdistribution.com

For E. A. P.

CONTENTS

FOREWORD   xv

INTRODUCTION   xix

1   A King Rides In   1

2   In the Beginning   7

3   Love Me Tender   21

4   Graceland   31

5   Flaming Star   41

6   My Kingdom for a Horse   55

7   Rising Sun   65

8   A New Beginning   75

9   Home at the Circle G   83

10   A Passion for Horses   93

11   Return to Reality   109

12   King of Hearts   121

13   The Man Called Charro   131

14   A True Performer   139

15   The King's Legacy   145

EPILOGUE   Coming Full Circle   153

WITH THANKS AND GRATITUDE   159

APPENDIX A   Partial List of Horses
Owned by Elvis Presley   161

APPENDIX B   Rising Sun   165

APPENDIX C   Key Events in the
Life of Elvis Presley   167

APPENDIX D   The Complete Films
of Elvis Presley   179

APPENDIX E   Pedigree of Elvis Presley's
Horse Rising Sun   182

BIBLIOGRAPHY   185

NOTES   189

"You have walked among us a spirit, and your shadow has been a light upon our faces."

—**KAHLIL GIBRAN**, *The Prophet*

FOREWORD

BY LARRY GELLER

Was Elvis Presley truly happy?

We were riding our horses at Elvis's Circle G Ranch on a warm summer afternoon in 1967, when Elvis brought his horse Rising Sun to a quick halt. He looked across the rolling green hills. "Larry, this ranch is my dream. I've been looking for something like this for a long time. You know how much I love singing and making records, and bein' in movies." He had an almost wistful, faraway look in his eyes. "But out here, riding our horses the way we are and livin' on the ranch close to Mother Nature—that's where it's at for me. I can't stand staying out in Hollyweird too long. It's so easy to lose yourself out there, and this place brings me back to the basics. I'm talkin' about hanging on to your soul."

Being true to oneself, staying in touch with the basics, was a meaningful theme like a golden thread that ran throughout Elvis's life. Those basics, what meant the most to him, were the pure joy of singing, the happiness he brought to his fans and, most of all, his little daughter Lisa Marie. Often, he would quote something his beloved mother drilled into him. "Never forget where you came from, and don't pretend to be something you're not." This became a central truth that he struggled to live up to his entire life. Thrust onto the world stage, rising from utter poverty to the heights of luxury and fame, Elvis was always humble and grateful for the blessings he had been given.

I thought I knew just about everything there was to know about Elvis Presley. I had worked for him, travelled with him, even sometimes lived at Graceland, and we were close personal friends. I even lived at the Circle G Ranch when he was there, where I witnessed first-hand his love and respect for horses. Yet, throughout the pages of this interesting, well-researched, and insightful book, I often found myself smiling or even laughing at something that was fresh and new to me. Whether you've been a fan your whole life, or just discovered the magic of Elvis, this book is a page-turner!

Elvis's life and career are legendary; he's been profiled and written about in many hundreds of books, more than any other entertainer or cultural icon in history. I am honored to have been asked by Kimberly Gatto and Victoria Racimo to write the foreword to their unique and intimate window into Elvis's extraordinary life.

Larry Geller

INTRODUCTION

"It's surprising how much you can look forward to the morning when there's a horse waiting on you."

—ELVIS PRESLEY

A well-worn adage states, "The outside of a horse is good for the inside of a man." Throughout history, time and again, these words have been proven true. Those of us who love horses share a unique, indelible bond with these profoundly God-like creatures. A soft muzzle, a playful nicker, or the sound of a contented horse munching hay can often soothe the most troubled of souls. One feels a sensation of peace, of quietude, if one allows a horse's loving spirit to enter the human heart. Riding a horse gives a sense of true freedom and a good gallop atop a fine steed can cure even the toughest of ills.

Receiving love from a horse is a gift. Elvis Presley discovered this to be true.

Elvis's great love of horses evolved in childhood, but owning a horse was a luxury that the Presleys were certainly unable to afford. Growing up in Southern poverty, Elvis quietly nurtured the dream that one day he would own a horse. As he began to earn money as a young star, Elvis frequently rented horses and rode with friends at a local dude ranch. At the height of his fame in the mid-1960s, Elvis Presley would find himself the proud owner of dozens of horses and two farms on which to take care of them. Most importantly, it was in this world of horses that he found the solace he so dearly sought. His horses took him away from the world that clamored for Elvis Presley, the superstar—a world that left him with little time to himself.

Video clips that remain to this day show a radiant and carefree Elvis amongst his horses. The footage reveals that Elvis was not merely a fan of horses, but also a skillful rider, with soft hands and seat, enjoying a true connection with his equine partner. A sense of peace and tranquility is evident on the singer's face. "Everyone knows Elvis and his music, his films, his charities, but they didn't know much about his true pastime," Priscilla Presley would later recall. "Elvis was happiest when riding horses."[1]

In the nearly forty years since Elvis's passing, countless books have been written about the star. These books seemingly chronicle every detail of his too-brief life, with subjects ranging from his movies to his favorite foods to his many relationships. This is the story of another, less familiar, side of Elvis Presley—the story of the King's love of horses.

As the old adage states, the outside of a horse became very good for the inside of a man. In this case, that man was none other than Elvis Aaron Presley.

1

A KING RIDES IN

As the sun rose from its nightly slumber, fans began to gather at the entrance of a stately abode. They clustered like leaves around the iron gates, which stood at the bottom of a long driveway. Some attempted to climb the grey stone walls that stood near the road, while others waited patiently. It was Memphis, Tennessee in the early 1970s and folks were united in their quest for a glimpse of the King.

Everett Brown was a young man on another type of mission on this warm summer's day. Driving to work, he had run into trouble with an overheated car that had placed him squarely on Bellevue Avenue. Brown headed towards the local phone booth to call a friend for help.

As he walked down the long road, Brown saw the familiar gates and walls of Graceland, the home of Elvis Presley.

Little did Brown know that, on that day, he was about to come face-to-face with the legend. As the young man peered up the long driveway, a unique figure caught his attention. There he was—Elvis—sitting atop a golden steed with a flowing white mane and tail. He wore white pants and a ruffled shirt and sported a purple scarf around his neck. Brown's eyes widened as the King effortlessly guided his Palomino, Rising Sun, down towards the gates. Brown found himself in the right place at the right time; Elvis Presley was riding down to greet his fans.

As the superstar mingled with the group that had assembled, Brown watched from afar, mesmerized by the sight. "I looked across the street, and sure enough, Elvis was crisscrossing the lawn on Rising Sun," Brown remembers. "He looked so majestic, as did the palomino horse he was riding."[1] Years later, Brown, a Tennessee-based singer/songwriter, would pen a song about his chance encounter with the King and his horse that shone, Brown wrote, "like a diamond in the delta dawn." The song, "Rising Sun," included the following stanza that eloquently described the scene:

Rising Sun was the horse's name
A palomino with a golden mane
A silver saddle and a flashing stride
A pony fit for a king to ride.

Aside from the local fans that stood outside for a glimpse of their idol, few outside Elvis's inner circle knew of his truly deep-seated passion for horses. This was, in many ways, a positive thing, as the stable was one of only a few scant areas where Elvis could escape from the pressures of his fame. At the height of his stardom, Elvis had difficulty even leaving his home without being mobbed by eager fans. In the barn and on the grounds, with his horses, he was able to find serenity, if only temporarily.

While Elvis enjoyed the peacefulness provided by his time with horses, he also delighted in sharing them with his beloved admirers. It is well-chronicled that Elvis adored his legions of fans, and he relished in sharing his love of horses with those he felt had supported him. He would often gallop "Sun" alongside the stone walls so that fans could watch the pair in action, then ride down to the gates. Elvis would sometimes spend hours at a time chatting with folks and signing autographs. On occasion, he would allow parents to prop their young children up on the horse with him, posing for photographs as both the parents and children grinned with joy.

Most of the time, during these rides, Elvis would be atop Rising Sun, but he could also be spotted riding his other favorite—Bear, a shiny, black, flat-shod Tennessee Walker. Over time, folks got to know the names and appearances of the horses, and Elvis enjoyed joking with them. On one summer morning, a woman asked Elvis if he'd be riding Bear later. The star laughingly replied, "No, honey, I think I'll keep my clothes on!"[2]

In such a way, the horses provided a dual purpose for Elvis. When he desired solace, he could slip into the barn and brush, talk to, or care for his horses without interruption. Some say he was more organized in the barn than in any other aspect of his life. He enjoyed cleaning tack, fixing fences, and grooming his horses until they gleamed. He labeled everything in the tack room; fans visiting Graceland today can see his handwriting on the walls where he labeled each horse's tack. While he often rode together with his wife Priscilla and with his group of friends known as the "Memphis Mafia," Elvis would just as frequently ride alone, sometimes saddling up his horse after breakfast and embarking on a few hours' worth of soul-searching.

Besides offering him a much-needed escape, horses also served the entertainer side of Elvis. If he planned to ride or put on a show for his fans near the gates or on the lawn at Graceland, he often dressed the part in stylish pants, a silk blouse, and a brightly colored scarf, or perhaps a black leather jacket and matching chaps, leather gloves, and a derby hat. Ever the showman, he would sometimes toss the scarf he was wearing to a lucky fan that stood nearby. When he rode alone or worked in the barn, Elvis typically wore a less formal outfit of jeans, a suede jacket, chaps, and a cowboy hat. In both instances—whether he was showing off for fans or finding an escape from the rigors of his fame—it is clear that Elvis appeared extremely happy and content when he was with his horses.

2

IN THE BEGINNING

While nearly every aspect of Elvis Presley's life has been widely chronicled in print, there is no evidence as to whether Elvis ever rode horses as a child. There is a likelihood he was exposed to horses in some remote way, as most children are given a pony ride at a local park or petting zoo. It is also possible that some folks in the Tupelo, Mississippi area, where Elvis lived as a young boy, would have owned working horses, along with cows, chickens, and other animals that are used in farming.

Growing up as the only child of Vernon and Gladys Presley—his twin, Jessie Garon, was stillborn—Elvis was an animal lover from the beginning. Vernon Presley remembered that Elvis had an affinity for all living creatures, even

Elvis had an affinity for all animals. He and co-star Dolores Hart are shown petting a calf in a publicity still from the film *Loving You* in 1957. *Photo courtesy of Paramount Studios.*

as a small child. "When he was a boy, I asked him to go hunting with me," Vernon later recalled. "But when he answered, 'Daddy, I don't want to kill birds,' I didn't try to persuade him to go against his feelings."[1]

There are references to dogs called "Woodlawn" and "Muffy Dee" in writings on Elvis's childhood, but it is unknown whether the Presleys actually owned these dogs or if they belonged to neighbors or friends. Vernon and Gladys Presley had chickens and roosters at their small property, and little Elvis bonded with them. According to some sources, two-year-old Elvis was reportedly inconsolable when his pet rooster passed away.[2] Horses, for obvious reasons, were more of a luxury than small pets and would not have been financially possible for the Presleys to own at that time.

Elvis's love of horses in particular was apparent by March of 1956, when he was photographed for the first time by the now famous Alfred Wertheimer at CBS Studios on Broadway in New York City. When Wertheimer walked into the room, Elvis was being fitted for a custom ring he had ordered several weeks prior. Wertheimer recalled, "Elvis was more interested in the ring than me, I was sort of breaking his train of thought.... So the ring salesman had just delivered this ring and Elvis put it on his finger and

Elvis's custom horseshoe ring is visible as the singer rides in the back of a car in New York City on June 29, 1956. © *Alfred Wertheimer / Premium Archive / Getty Images.*

he liked it. It turned out to be a horseshoe ring with diamonds all around the horseshoe and a horse's head going across the shoe itself."[3]

Interestingly, while visiting Memphis many years later, Wertheimer noticed a bronze statue of Elvis in a small park. The statue depicted Elvis holding a guitar in one hand, with the opposite arm outstretched. Wertheimer recalled, "Sure enough, what was on that finger of the other hand? It was the horseshoe ring with the diamonds and the horse's head except now it was two inches in diameter and it was made out of bronze rather than diamonds and gold."[4]

The first recorded proof of Elvis actually riding horses dates back to 1955, when he was a young man of twenty. At that time, Elvis was dating June Juanico, a lovely young woman who lived with her family in Biloxi, Mississippi. In her book, *Elvis in the Twilight of Memory*, June recalled that Elvis—still a youth on the brink of stardom—daydreamed about someday having horses of his own. After driving by several ranches, Elvis said to June, "I guess I'll just have to buy one of my own, huh?" and later commented that it would be nice to have a ranch with horses.[5]

During the course of their relationship (which spanned 1955 and 1956), Elvis and June sometimes vacationed at the Gulf Hills Resort in Ocean Springs, Mississippi. It has been reported that Elvis and his family had begun visiting

Gulf Hills as far back as 1951. The resort, originally established in 1927, boasted a colorful history, serving as a place of respite for Chicago gangsters such as Al Capone and, later, entertainers like Judy Garland and Fats Domino. The property included an assortment of villas, a sprawling golf course, water for swimming and fishing, and a clubhouse with a lounge that carried the moniker "The Pink Pony." While Elvis was not a drinker, he was known to spend many evenings at the lounge, where he enjoyed singing and playing piano for friends and patrons of the ranch.

The Gulf Hills Resort had added horseback riding to its offerings only a short time before Elvis's first visit. Gulf Hills had decided to capitalize on the western "dude ranch" concept that was popular at that time, in which everyday folks were given a taste of the old "Wild West." Management built a stable and purchased a herd of twenty-plus saddle horses, which would enable the resort's guests to explore the miles of trails that spanned the property. According to a 1950 article in the *Times–Picayne* newspaper, "a half dozen cowhands were imported from west Texas to provide riding instruction and to supervise group outings" for guests at Gulf Hills. Additional activities on the 700-acre ranch included moonlight rides, hayrides, square dancing, campfire singing, and breakfast trail rides.[6]

Along with June Juanico and several of their friends, Elvis spent a substantial amount of time at Gulf Hills in the summer of 1956. At that time, Elvis was an up-and-coming star, having reached number one on the charts with his first RCA hit, "Heartbreak Hotel." The seclusion of the ranch offered Elvis an escape from his ever-growing legion of fans and also from the media, who tracked his every move. According to records, Elvis stayed at Gulf Hills on at least six different occasions during this time, and was, in fact, at the ranch when "Hound Dog" was released in July 1956. On occasion, Elvis's parents accompanied him to Gulf Hills for a family vacation.

June Juanico treasures her memories of riding with Elvis, and noted that Elvis even liked to sing while on horseback. In her memoir, June recalled one such ride:

> Our seven horses were saddled up and ready to ride. Elvis didn't like the idea of having a guide, but unless you knew the correct route, one wrong turn and the lead horse would make a run back to the stable, with the rest of the horses following. The next time out, our guide promised, we could go it alone.
>
> We left the stable in single file. Our guide was in front, Elvis was behind him, I was behind

Elvis, and so on down the line. We started off walking, then broke into a little trot, and then a nice canter. The guide's horse was slinging mud in Elvis's face, and Elvis's horse was slinging mud in my face—everyone was getting their share.

The canter was soon a full-fledged gallop, everyone racing for the front. It was like a mad day at the racetrack, with seven inexperienced jockeys going for pole position. Finally, we slowed to a walk. Everyone, apart from the guide, was covered in mud. We were laughing at each other, and Elvis, wiping his mouth on his shirt sleeve, started singing.

We didn't run the horses anymore; we were happy just to walk through the tall pines, singing.[7]

The singing on horseback became a regular occurrence for Elvis, and the horses provided a way for him to unwind and relax. June described another such ride as follows:

Singing and walking through the woods, we stretched the forty-five minute ride to ninety minutes. Thinking we were lost, one of the guides came looking for us, and we bumped into him

Elvis and girlfriend June Juanico embark on one of their summer trail rides at the Gulf Hills Dude Ranch in Mississippi in the mid-1950s. *Photo from the Russ Howe Collection.*

as we rounded the curve heading back to the stable. "That's enough action for today, gang. Let's go home and relax," Elvis said, thanking the horse with a pat on the neck.[8]

Since his time spent at the ranch was meant to be private, photographs of Elvis at Gulf Hills are scarce. However, on one occasion, when the group was saddled up and ready to embark on a trail ride, an onlooker snapped two photographs of young Elvis on horseback. In one black-and-white photo, Elvis sat astride a blaze-faced roan beside June, who was riding a Palomino in Western tack. In the other photograph, Elvis sits atop the same roan horse, while his friend Red West rides a darker white-faced horse. The two horses' muzzles were nearly touching when the photograph was snapped. A third photo, which shows Elvis and June standing arm-in-arm beside a horse in a paddock, would be featured in some fan magazines at that time.

Donna Brown, a contemporary manager of the resort, noted the importance of this time in young Elvis's life. "Gulf Hills was a secluded location back in the day," she said. "And it became his summer sanctuary. Elvis loved riding the horses, and he could be heard singing to no one in particular as they rode down the trail."[9]

Elvis and June Juanico enjoyed spending time with the horses at the Gulf Hills Dude Ranch in the mid-1950s. *Photo from the Russ Howe Collection.*

Cecil "Ces" Spearman, who was a young, recently discharged U.S. Marine Corps officer in the mid-1950s, was working at the ranch when Elvis visited. Spearman led Elvis and his friends on a guided trail ride on at least one occasion. While Spearman, in his recollections, did not specifically mention Elvis's interaction with the horses, he was quick to remember the singer's kindness. Years later, Spearman recalled that Elvis would spend hours at a time signing autographs and posing with fans, despite the fact that he was on vacation.[10] This willingness of Elvis to spend time with his fans, at the expense of his privacy, would continue for the remainder of his lifetime.

Elvis's time at the Gulf Hills dude ranch came to an end in 1957, and, sadly, so did his relationship with June Juanico. Elvis's ever-growing stardom and frequent travel made the relationship difficult to sustain, and the two parted ways, with only fond memories remaining. When Elvis bumped into June many years later after a concert in Las Vegas in the 1970s, he had many questions for her. Interestingly, one of the first questions he asked of June was whether she had horses.[11]

The time spent at the Gulf Hills ranch represented a happy, idyllic period in Elvis's life. It was a period of innocence in which the world ahead of him held great promise, and fame had not yet become overwhelming. The ranch, and the horses there, brought Elvis a sense of peace—one that he would never forget and would seek out later in his life.

3

LOVE ME TENDER

Given Elvis's love for horses, it is fitting that the first time he appeared on a movie screen was in a traditional Western film. The film, called *Love Me Tender*, gave fans their first view of their idol as an actor when it was released in November of 1956. Besides gaining his first experience as an actor, Elvis would also begin to hone his equestrian skills in *Love Me Tender*. During the course of production, Elvis would be filmed not only riding horses, but also ground driving a team and manning a horse-drawn cart.

Originally entitled *The Reno Brothers*, *Love Me Tender* was intended as a vehicle for a more established film actor; in fact, it has been reported that both Robert Wagner and Jeffrey Hunter had turned down the role before it was offered to Elvis. On March 26, 1956, while he was still dating June Juanico, Elvis screen-tested for director Hal Wallis at Paramount Studios in Hollywood, California. Wallis was famous for having produced such classic films as *Casablanca* and *The Maltese Falcon* and had worked with some of Hollywood's legendary leading men, including Humphrey Bogart and Errol Flynn.

Elvis's screen test lasted three days, during which he performed scenes from both *The Rainmaker* and William Inge's *The Girls of Summer*. The young man's test impressed onlookers, including Wallis's partner, Joe Hazen, who noted Elvis's "great potentialities" as an actor. A week later, Wallis offered Elvis a contract for one film, with options for an additional six motion pictures; the contract also stipulated that Elvis was free to make at least one motion picture per year for another studio. Wallis, unable to find a suitable role for Elvis at that time, agreed that summer to loan the budding actor to Twentieth Century Fox Studios for filming of *The Reno Brothers*.

Elvis was to play Clint Reno, the youngest of three brothers working on the family farm in Texas in the years following the American Civil War. Noted actor Richard Egan portrayed Elvis's older brother Vance, a Confederate soldier who returns home after several years, while

Debra Paget played Clint's troubled young wife, Cathy. June Juanico wrote that Elvis was reluctant to accept the role of Clint Reno when he realized that his character would be killed at the end of the film. Nevertheless, he relented, and put his heart and soul into performing the role. Allegedly, Elvis arrived for filming having already memorized all of his lines, as well as the lines for all the other characters.

Portions of *Love Me Tender*, including the horse-related scenes, were filmed at the Twentieth Century Fox Ranch in Calabasas, California, and the Bell Moving Picture Ranch in the state's Santa Susana Mountains. Movie ranches such as these were developed in the 1920s and were ideal for location shooting on Western films in Southern California. Outside of the typical confines of a studio, these sites offered rustic valleys, foothills, and canyons that provided both a natural backdrop and ample space for action-packed scenes involving horseback riding and shooting.

Frank Klump, a legendary horse trainer and wrangler in Hollywood, was assigned the task of managing the equine scenes in *Love Me Tender*. Klump specialized in training animals for movies and TV, and, according to his daughter, Candy, "taught countless actors how to stay aboard a horse."[1] These included James Dean, Gregory Peck, and other screen stars. One of the most memorable for him, however, was Elvis, whom he coached during the horse-related scenes in *Love Me Tender*.

Well-respected stuntwoman Martha Crawford Cantarini, who worked as a double for Debra Paget in *Love Me Tender*, remembers Elvis as a "sweet, kind, country boy" who loved horses and enjoyed hearing stories about the various equines used in the film. In her memoir, *Fall Girl*, Cantarini recalled, "Elvis and I talked about Jim, the horse I had been using to double the cast horse for the chase scenes, and about the horse Debra Paget was riding—a sweet, kind, gentle creature owned by Jimmy Loucks, the rimrod wrangler."[2]

According to Cantarini, Elvis appeared to have some riding experience at the time—most likely from his trail riding days at Gulf Hills—but did not appear to have had any formal riding instruction. That being said, he took easily to both the riding and driving scenes for the film. The work would be grueling, with some of the more physical segments taking hours to complete under the torrid August sun. During breaks from filming, Elvis would sit with Cantarini under the shade of a nearby tree and talk about horses. Elvis delighted in hearing about the antics of the stuntwoman's own horse, Frosty, a brilliant Palomino she

While he had ridden in the past, Elvis honed his riding skills in preparation for his first film, the Western *Love Me Tender*. Here he is shown on set in the role of Clint Reno. *Photo courtesy of Photofest Inc.*

had raised from foalhood. With a large personality and a knack for mischief, Frosty had figured out how to unlock the stable doors and let himself—and the other horses—out of the barn in the middle of the night. Frosty's penchant for tricks would prove valuable in his later career with Cantarini, as the horse would star in numerous television commercials and other appearances in the 1960s and 70s, including shows at the famous Thunderbird Hotel in Las Vegas.

Filming *Love Me Tender* with live animals was not without challenge for Elvis. As a novice-level horseman at that time, Elvis was still learning about the quirks and unpredictability of the large, majestic creatures weighing 1,000 pounds or more. Memorabilia collector Jim Curtin, who later became a friend to Elvis, recalled a particularly humbling experience for Elvis involving horses on the set of the film:

> Elvis had to learn how to ride a horse like an expert for *Love Me Tender.* He told both his producer and director that he already knew how to ride and would be able to get through the scenes without looking foolish.
>
> One scene required Elvis to ride his horse through grass and trees. When the test run for the shot went well, the director called for a real take. Elvis mounted and maneuvered his horse

through the field just as he had before, and everything went smoothly until they neared some tree
limbs. His horse stopped listening to commands
and ran straight into the limbs, knocking Elvis

Elvis and his manager, Colonel Tom Parker, are shown with a team of horses on
the set of *Love Me Tender* in 1956. *Photo courtesy of Photofest Inc.*

off. He slid from the horse and rolled over, landing several feet away.

Elvis got slowly to his feet and shook his head. When he took a step, he lost his balance. He walked slowly to his dressing room, dusting the dirt off his clothes. He was so embarrassed at being knocked off the horse that he slipped into the stables later that day, looked his horse square in the eye, and scolded him. The horse whinnied and snorted and pushed Elvis away with his head. Elvis was unaware that two crew members witnessed him scolding the animal. They laughed at the sight, and then went back and told everyone what they had seen. Elvis was embarrassed twice that day![3]

Filming for *Love Me Tender* wrapped on September 21, 1956, with the movie opening at the box office less than eight weeks later. Critical reviews of the film were mixed, but Elvis received considerable praise from his loyal fans for his first attempt as a movie actor. Meanwhile, Elvis performed the title track from the film for the first time in public when he appeared on *The Ed Sullivan Show* during a break from filming on September 9. A mere two weeks later, it was announced by RCA that advanced sales of the

In this shot from the film *Loving You*, Elvis (as Deke Rivers) leans against a paddock fence as horses graze nearby. *Photo courtesy of Paramount Studios.*

song had resulted in it reaching gold status before the movie was released—something that had never happened before.

Elvis's next film, *Loving You*, did not require him to be on horseback. However, in one scene from the film, Elvis—as character Deke Rivers—runs up to a paddock of horses and leans back against a fence while conversing with co-star Dolores Hart. That would be the extent of his on-screen equine endeavors until 1960 in *Flaming Star*, the second traditional Western film in which Elvis would appear. In the meantime, the future King would purchase a castle—one at which horses would be very much at home.

4

GRACELAND

By the time *Love Me Tender* was released in late 1956, Elvis Presley had become an unmistakable household name. His celebrity status had become so widespread that fans and media surrounded the home he shared with his parents, as they hoped for any glimpse of the young star. Fans camped outside his home at 1034 Audubon Drive in Memphis at all hours of the day and night, even when Elvis was not there. This constant fan presence offered no sense of privacy for the Presleys or for those who lived nearby. When neighbors repeatedly complained about the constant stream of boisterous commotion, Elvis decided to purchase a more private residence for himself and his beloved parents.

In early 1957, while Elvis was filming *Loving You*, he instructed Vernon and Gladys to search for a home of their liking, with a budget of approximately $100,000 to spend. According to some reports, Elvis requested that his parents specifically look for a "farmhouse" type property, perhaps with the intent that he would be able to keep farm animals there. In mid-March, Vernon and Gladys visited Graceland, a stately Georgian-style colonial mansion located in Whitehaven, Tennessee, which then had a population of 5,000. At the time, the thirteen-acre estate was surrounded by open land, which would subsequently be developed into residential areas as Memphis's urban areas expanded.

Graceland had originated as "Graceland Farms," a 500-acre parcel owned by the family of Stephen Toof. A printer by trade, Toof had founded the oldest commercial printing company in the area and had also served as the pressroom foreman of the *Memphis Daily Appeal* newspaper. According to lore, the farm was named in honor of Toof's daughter, Grace, who inherited the property in 1894. Following the death of Grace Toof, ownership of the farm passed on to her niece, Ruth Moore, an area socialite and wife of Memphis physician Thomas Moore.

At the time when the Moores gained ownership of the property, Graceland Farms had been used primarily for the breeding and sales of Hereford cattle and did not include a residential home. The Moores constructed the two-story Graceland mansion in 1939, at which time it measured 10,266 square feet, having been designed by Memphis architects Furbringer and Ehrman. Interestingly, the Graceland home harbored a musical connection from the beginning, as the Moores' daughter was a harpist with the Memphis Symphony Orchestra and often utilized the mansion's front rooms for classical recitals.

By 1957, the property had been subdivided, with the mansion and several acres of surrounding land being offered for sale; the remaining acreage, still known as Graceland Farms, was not included in the purchase. Accompanied by a real estate agent at their visit, Gladys and Vernon Presley were immediately taken with Graceland's pastoral beauty and peaceful surroundings. When Elvis checked in with his parents, they explained their affection for the Graceland property.

During a break from filming *Jailhouse Rock*, Elvis visited Graceland himself and was similarly enamored with the attractiveness and privacy offered by its long driveway, trees, and open land. That spring, twenty-two-year-old Elvis purchased the Graceland home and surrounding grounds for just over $100,000. Vernon and Gladys moved into their new residence on May 16, 1957. However, as Elvis was in the midst of filming a movie in California, he would not join his parents in residence at the family home until June 26.

While the mansion was vacant at the time of its purchase by the Presleys, the grounds included a small stable that had been used by Graceland's previous owners. Upon moving to the property, Vernon and Gladys reportedly had several farm animals living there, including chickens and pigs—the latter being used by Vernon to produce smoked pork and bacon. The family also owned donkeys, which were allegedly stabled in the drained-out swimming pool for a brief time before fencing was installed. It has been speculated that the family kept a horse or two in the barn during their early years there; however, there are no definitive reports that the Presleys owned horses at this time.

Sara Erwin, who grew up on the property adjacent to the parcel owned by Elvis, noted that the land surrounding Elvis's property in the late 1950s was primarily equestrian in nature. The larger Graceland Farms property included several areas for riding and boarding horses, and, to that end, boasted several paddocks, pastures, and a larger barn. It also included the Graceland Farms Stable Club, a riding club for children that was founded in 1952 by William N. Spence. Known as "Mr. Bill," Spence managed the stables and riding programs for Graceland Farms and also served as an announcer at local horse shows. Spence was no stranger to the Graceland mansion, as he had tended to the horses of the estate's previous owners.

In her memoir, *Over the Fence*, Erwin explained:

> Back then, Graceland was 140 acres of rolling pasture land, home to prized cattle and horses. In 1957 when the owners decided to sell the house and subdivide the land, Elvis bought the mansion and a few acres. Before the rest of the land was subdivided, the real estate company permitted a few people to board horses there at Graceland Farms. My parents paid five dollars a month to keep our horses in the big white barn that is still a landmark at Graceland.[1]

Erwin recalled that when Elvis realized that the surrounding property was soon to be subdivided, he made a second purchase that included "a few more acres and the big barn." At the time, the stalls were being leased to several boarders, including Erwin, who stabled their horses there and rode around the extensive grounds. At the time, there was no fence surrounding Elvis's property, which allowed the young riders the unique opportunity of observing the activities of their famous new neighbor. Erwin and her friends gained a key glimpse into Elvis's life at that time as he happily drove a tractor around the property and enjoyed the simpler aspects of farming. As privacy became an issue, Elvis would later arrange for the construction of a fence around the property, as well as the stone wall and decorative iron gates at the entrance to the driveway that have since become world-famous.

Though decades have passed, Erwin has fond memories of Elvis, who would, as a young man, show great interest in expanding his knowledge of horses. Often, the teens who boarded at Graceland Farms would loan a horse to their famous neighbor so that Elvis could go riding along with the group. "We showed Elvis every feature we had discovered about the barn," Erwin wrote in her memoir, "Including a secret storage room through a small door in the corner of the barn. Elvis was impressed with how many stalls there were there and with the sheer vastness of the storage rooms and the huge hayloft."[2] She noted the wonder on the young singer's face when he was informed that one of the mares was due to foal, and described his curiosity with regard to the various breeds and personalities of the teenagers' horses. "He asked questions about which of the horses in the stalls were quarter horses, which were gaited saddle horses, and if any were stallions," she said. He also seemed intrigued with the automatic waterer that filled the troughs on a regular basis, ensuring that the horses would always have fresh water.

Soon this idyllic period would come to an end since Elvis had to return to film-making; his manager, the colorful "Colonel" Tom Parker, was eager to keep the star earning money. While he was away, construction continued on the Graceland property, as it was necessary to provide privacy for the Presleys.

As a testament to his compassion for others, Erwin remembered that Elvis seemed bothered by the fact that, with the change in ownership, the teens were about to be displaced from the barn they so loved. He expressed a deep empathy for others and did not want to hurt anyone. Erwin recalled that Elvis suggested that the teens could perhaps remain as boarders in the stable, which was later found to be impossible as the stalls would be needed for his own horses. "He seemed sensitive that he was causing us to lose this fine place to keep our horses," she wrote. "Of course, it was impossible to share the barn even though it was a genuine gesture of friendship from Elvis." Similarly, when Elvis later discovered that the construction of the fence around his property had cut off the water supply to the old Graceland Farms, he "allowed the manager of Graceland Farms to divert water to the horse troughs without paying for the water."[3]

The Graceland Farms land where the boarding stables had been was later subdivided into several parcels for the construction of residential homes. Erwin and her family built a home on one such parcel, which meant that she continued in her role as Elvis's neighbor. Meanwhile, in December 1957, Elvis received a draft notice for military service. While his celebrity status afforded him the chance to enlist in Special Services as an entertainer for the troops, Elvis opted instead to serve as a regular soldier.

Elvis was originally scheduled for induction into the Army on January 20, 1958; however, he requested and was granted an extension in order to complete work on the movie *King Creole*, which was in production at that time. After filming was completed, Elvis was sworn into the U.S. Army on March 24, 1958 at Fort Chaffee, Arkansas. There he spent four days before being transferred to Fort Hood in Texas for basic training, leaving behind his superstar status to be treated the same as any other soldier.

This time of upheaval in Elvis's life was made even more difficult when his mother, Gladys, became seriously ill in August of that year. As Gladys's condition took a turn for the worse, Elvis was granted emergency leave to visit with his mother on August 12. Sadly, Gladys Presley died of a heart attack a mere two days later, leaving Elvis utterly heartbroken. The death of his beloved mother was a tragedy that wounded Elvis deeply; it was an event from which, many believe, he never fully recovered.

Following the tragic loss of his mother, Elvis was assigned to leave the United States and serve in Germany, where he would spend the next two years of his young life. During his time in the Army, Elvis was to meet several folks who would become close friends for the remainder of his life, including Joe Esposito, who later was his road manager, and budding singer Charlie Hodge, who would perform with Elvis on stage. And in Germany in September 1959, Elvis would meet young Priscilla Beaulieu, the woman who would later become his wife.

While horses were not a prominent part of Elvis's life while he served as a soldier in the Army, photographs taken during this time illustrate the deep affection that he still had for the animals. In March 1959, Colonel Parker and RCA had arranged for a photo shoot in an effort to keep Elvis visible to fans while serving his country overseas. The session included several memorable pictures of Elvis, clad in his Army uniform, standing alongside a team of bay carriage horses in front of the Dankeskirche church in Bad Nauheim. These photographs make the sense of love and respect that Elvis had for horses abundantly clear. Interestingly, Colonel Parker chose one of the photographs of Elvis with horses for use on a Christmas card he would send out that year.

Following his return to the U.S. after completion of his Army service in March 1960, Elvis immediately returned to film-making. Fittingly, the first film he made during this period was the military musical *G.I. Blues*, in which he starred opposite dancer/actress Juliet Prowse. Following the completion of that film, Elvis would begin work on *Flaming Star*, the second of three traditional Westerns he would star in during his lifetime.

5

FLAMING STAR

As cameras roll in the opening scenes of 1960's *Flaming Star*, Elvis sits tall upon the back of a flashy white-faced chestnut horse, galloping across the screen in glorious Technicolor. Throughout the film, Elvis appeared every inch the confident horseman in his role as the Native American cowboy Pacer Burton. While certain action segments for the film were performed by veteran stunt double Tom Sweet, Elvis completed many of the basic riding scenes himself. Elvis would be filmed on horseback in both the opening and closing scenes, as well as in various parts of the movie. Similar to his role in *Love Me Tender*, Elvis would also be required to drive a horse-drawn cart in a couple of scenes.

On August 1, 1960, Elvis arrived on set at Twentieth Century Fox Studios for preproduction work on the film, which was referred to at the time as *Flaming Lance* after the book on which it was based. The film would undergo several title metamorphoses—subsequently being renamed *Black Star* before ultimately being released as *Flaming Star*. (Elvis's version of the former title track, "Black Star," was ultimately released in 1991 on the CD *Elvis: Collectors Gold*.)

Elvis played Pacer Burton, the son of a Kiowa mother and a Texan father, who is trapped between the conflicting worlds of the Native Americans and the white settlers. In order to play the role of a half Native American man, blue-eyed Elvis was originally fitted with brown contact lenses for the film; however, this idea was later scrapped. Prior to filming, Elvis was given two weeks' worth of riding lessons to hone his skills in the saddle. The lessons, under the tutelage of the studio wrangler, began on August 2 and took place every afternoon.

Upon arriving on set, Elvis appeared to be a fairly confident rider. "Elvis could ride extremely well," recalled co-star Barbara Eden, who later earned worldwide fame as the star of the television show *I Dream of Jeannie*.[1] In an interview with author Alanna Nash in 2008, Eden said of Elvis, "He was a natural on a horse. He was really good at it, as he was at acting."[2]

A shirtless Elvis in an action scene involving horses from the Western *Flaming Star*. *Photo courtesy of Photofest Inc.*

No matter how self-assured a rider may be, a single incident with a rogue horse is often enough to shake that core sense of confidence when mounted. In that regard, Elvis was no different than any other horseman. Lamar Fike, a close friend of Elvis's, recalled how an incident during the filming of *Flaming Star* would rock the star's confidence in the saddle:

> In August '60, we were out on the set of *Flaming Star*, and Elvis and this big wrangler named Jim went riding over in the back streets where the western set was. Elvis was getting acquainted with the horse he was going to ride in the movie, when the horse decided he wanted to go back to the barn.
>
> We were just sitting there, when out of the blue, here came Elvis. His horse was just wide open, and the wrangler was nowhere in sight.
>
> There was a road with asphalt pavement, and a gate and a fence and a lot of things you could run into and get hurt pretty bad if you were on top of a runaway horse. And the horse turned to go down this road, his legs went one way, and Elvis, hanging on, was pretty much leaning on the other. Well, that horse came running underneath

the gate. If Elvis had not ducked, he would have decapitated himself. After Elvis ducked, the horse got to his stall and stopped on a dime. Elvis sat there a minute, just as white as a sheet, and then he climbed off. He never let go of the reins.

Just then, Jim, the wrangler, showed up. Jim said, "Mr. Presley, I am so sorry about this. I do not know what happened…" He said, "Mr. Presley, I will have another horse out here for you tomorrow."

And Elvis said, "No, no. I want him."

And that's the horse Elvis rode in *Flaming Star*.[3]

While this incident surely shook Elvis's feelings of security on horseback, the star did not reveal any anxiety when he appeared onscreen. Throughout the film he is shown mounting and dismounting from horses and riding at all three gaits, exuding the confidence and swagger of a real cowboy. Film critic A. H. Weiler, in his *New York Times* review of the film, noted that, "(Presley) sits a horse well and is properly brave and stoic."[4]

In one scene from the original taping, Elvis sings the song "Britches" while on horseback. "Britches" (along with another song, "Summer Kisses, Winter Tears") would be cut from the final film after test-showings revealed that audiences found the scene to be too stale for their liking. Allegedly Elvis was pleased with this news, as he too found the idea of a cowboy singing while in the saddle to be rather corny. In the final release, Elvis would sing only two songs in the film (rather than the usual six to eight), which encouraged him in his quest to play fewer musical comedy parts and more serious, non-singing roles.

While Elvis rode a chestnut horse in much of the film, he also rode a large Appaloosa in later scenes. Near the end of the movie, Elvis's character Pacer Burton—having been mortally wounded—sees the "flaming star of death" and rides the Appaloosa back to the family ranch for a final farewell. Accepting his fate, the bleeding Pacer then gallops off into the mountains, presumably to die.

Flaming Star, while often regarded as the best of the three traditional Westerns in which Elvis would appear, received only mixed reviews when it premiered at box offices in December of 1960. Opening a mere month after the release of *G.I. Blues*, *Flaming Star* did not achieve the box-office success garnered by the wartime musical comedy. In *Variety* magazine's list of top-grossing films for the year, *GI Blues* reached a respectable fourteenth spot, while *Flaming Star* remained nearer to the bottom of the list. This likely convinced Colonel Tom Parker that musical comedies, and not serious roles, would be the biggest money-makers for his

Publicity shot from *Flaming Star* with Elvis starring as Pacer Burton, a man torn between the two worlds of his white father and Kiowa mother. *Photo courtesy of Photofest Inc.*

star. In such a way, the ending of *Flaming Star*, with a wounded Elvis riding off into the mountains to die alone, was somewhat synonymous with the direction of his film career and his feelings about it at the time. He would simply acquiesce to the demands presented to him.

Following the release of *Flaming Star*, Elvis would not appear in another true Western for a period of nine long years. He did, however, make an appearance on horseback in the 1961 film, *Blue Hawaii*, albeit only in one brief scene. Midway through the film, Elvis—as tour guide Chad Gates—leads a group on horseback through the beaches of Kauai as the song "Island of Love" plays in the background. Elvis looks quite relaxed in the scene, as he does in a production still where he rests on the horse's neck while speaking to a member of the crew.

Darlene Tompkins, who co-starred in *Blue Hawaii*, remembers that scene with vivid emotion. The movie, as she recalls, was completed in one month, with indoor scenes shot at Paramount Studios and the outdoor scenes filmed on location in Hawaii. Tompkins remembers that Elvis was riding a beautiful, black horse with a gleaming coat that shined brightly in the Hawaiian sun. As they practiced the scene with the horses, the black horse acted up with Elvis on his back, rearing up on its hind legs as it aggressively approached one of the other horses, a mare ridden by actress Pamela Austin. The frightened actress fell forward and landed on the horse's mane before being assisted by on-site wranglers, who helped her to dismount. Meanwhile, despite being jostled in the saddle on the rearing horse, Elvis maintained control of the animal so that it did not harm the other horse. The black horse lost its balance, nearly falling to the ground, before Elvis was able to jump off. The movie wranglers and Elvis's entourage came to assist him, finding that both the star and the horse were uninjured.

When the scene was ultimately filmed, Austin was given a different horse to ride; Elvis, however, rode the same black horse that had given him difficulty during the practice scene. Tompkins recalled that the star seemed supremely confident and relaxed, even sliding his feet back in the stirrups and leaning back with one hand loosely holding the reins as they walked along the sandy trail. As Tompkins was riding the horse that was directly behind Elvis, she was able to observe the star's demeanor up close. "He was very relaxed, looking at the scenery", she remembers. "He had complete, absolute control of that horse."[5]

As the horses were stabled in an area away from the set, Elvis was unable to interact much with the animals during filming due to time constraints. "He would pet the horses when we got on and off, but there was not time for anything more," Tompkins recalled, as the wranglers came and took the horses as soon as the scene was completed.

Tompkins remembers the time she spent with Elvis with great fondness. As the two sat on lawn chairs between takes, she recalled, "He told me his dreams. He wanted to be a dramatic actor and to do stage work, which, sadly, he never got to do."[6] *Blue Hawaii* was a tremendous commercial success, which drove Colonel Parker to sign the star to even more musical comedies, and fewer dramatic roles, in the years to come.

Following *Blue Hawaii*, Elvis would star in a whopping fourteen films during the five-year period from 1961 through 1966. That being said, only two of these films included scenes that involved Elvis with horses. In the 1965 comedy *Tickle Me*, which received poor reviews, a horse appears to sing a line or two of the song "Dirty Dirty Feeling." Elvis performed the song in a stable, feeding hay to horses while singing, dancing, and, of course, being surrounded by a bevy of beautiful women. It was a far cry from the dramatic roles that Elvis yearned for as an actor.

The year 1965 also saw the release of the similarly disappointing *Harum Scarum*, in which Elvis starred as

Johnny Tyrone, a matinee idol who travels to the Middle East for the premiere of his latest film. While there, Johnny woos the beautiful Princess Shalimar, who was played by actress Mary Ann Mobley. The Mississippi-born Mobley had earned worldwide fame when she was crowned Miss America in 1958.

Harum Scarum was shot in twenty-eight days, during which director Sam Katzman was continuously looking to cut costs. That plan included using the actors in place of stunt doubles wherever possible, such as in the horse-back riding scene. Mobley later recalled, "The script said, 'Princess Shalimar gallops across the landscape on the back of an Arabian stallion, with her long hair and veils flying in the wind.' Mr. Sam called me into his office and asked if I rode a horse, and when I said I did, he said, 'Good, we don't have to hire a stunt double.' The horse was no pussycat, however. I go out to the horse and there is an old wrangler out there, chewin' and whittlin', and he looks up at me with all this orange chiffon on, and he says, 'You ridin' this horse?' And I said, 'Yessir.' And he said, 'Just remember one thing—it ain't my idea.' And that horse took off like lightning. That horse never had four feet on the ground the whole time I was riding. Elvis was saying, 'Slow down, Mary Ann.' I thought, 'This is gonna be embarrassing, when they pick me off the limb of a tree.'"[7]

In the horseback scene from *Harum Scarum*, Elvis appears confident and relaxed as he rides a stunning black horse through the countryside. However, it would be his last appearance on horseback in a film until the Western-themed comedy *Stay Away, Joe*, which would be filmed in late 1967.

In looking at the content of films such as *Tickle Me* and *Harum Scarum*, among others, it is easy to understand why Elvis was feeling frustrated with his career. Most of these films followed a similar formula: Elvis meets a girl, sings a few songs, loses said girl, sings more songs, and wins the girl back. While Elvis longed to play challenging roles on screen that would showcase his skills as an actor, he instead was forced to take on roles where he was filmed singing to dogs, horses, bulls, and puppets, among other things—scenes that any serious actor would find degrading. Elvis, who possessed a deep, intelligent soul, loved making movies, but found many of his experiences in Hollywood to be inauthentic and shallow. Elvis's cousin Billy Smith recalled, "He was discouraged about the quality of his movies. He said they were all just alike, basically. He wanted stronger roles. But his movies made money, and Colonel didn't want to change the format."[8] With such frustrations clouding his mind, Elvis was in need of something to help him feel grounded.

MY KINGDOM
FOR A HORSE

While Elvis had ridden various horses both in his personal life and on film, his passion for all things equine would reach new heights on a winter's day in 1966. It was a week before Christmas, and, in the spirit of the season, Elvis had come up with a surprise gift for his soon-to-be wife, Priscilla Beaulieu. Priscilla had long enjoyed riding horses and often expressed a wish to have a horse of her own. Elvis, whose thoughtfulness and generosity knew no bounds, thought a horse would be the perfect gift to make his fiancée smile.

Armed with this idea in mind, Elvis telephoned his friend Jerry Schilling, inviting him over to Graceland for breakfast. As the two men dined on traditional Southern fare, Elvis spoke to Jerry about his desire to purchase a horse for Priscilla. There was one caveat, however: Elvis wanted to know if he could also gift a horse to Jerry's fiancée, Sandy Kawelo (whom Jerry had met on the set of Elvis's film *Paradise, Hawaiian Style*). Elvis's reasoning was that Priscilla and Sandy could ride around the grounds of Graceland together, and he wanted to ensure that Jerry would be accepting of the idea. Jerry agreed in full, and the two men set off on their first of many horse-shopping expeditions.

The journey took place in an old, black, double-cab pickup truck, a vehicle that Elvis enjoyed driving as it offered him some much-needed anonymity. Few would expect to see the glamorous superstar driving a battered old truck; with his cowboy hat pulled down slyly over his forehead, Elvis was even less recognizable.

Bundled together in the pickup truck with Elvis at the wheel, the pair headed for the farm of "Mr. Bill" Spence, who was offering several horses for sale at the time. When the two men arrived at the farm, Jerry found that he, and not Elvis, was to be the test rider. Perhaps Elvis harbored some lingering fears after being run away with, and nearly injured, on the set of *Flaming Star*. Or perhaps he wanted to see how the horses would behave with a complete novice in the saddle. Whatever the reason, Elvis suggested that

Schilling test ride the sale horses and assist with choosing the proper mounts for Priscilla and Sandy. Schilling, who admittedly had no horse experience whatsoever at that time, was a good sport for the sake of his friend. And Elvis, whose sense of humor was legendary, appeared to fully enjoy the experience.

"I was sitting on horse after horse at farm after farm," Schilling wrote in his memoir *Me and a Guy Named Elvis*, "Just getting bounced around and trying like hell to stay on. And the harder I tried to stay on, the harder Elvis laughed. I started to get the feeling that he wasn't even really looking at the horses any more—he was just laughing his head off watching me."[1]

After several such trips to area stables, Elvis decided upon a four-year-old black quarter horse gelding named Domino for Priscilla and a sorrel mare called Sheba for Sandy. The gifts were tremendously successful; both women loved their new horses and rode around the grounds at Graceland nearly every day. Elvis, for his part, dove headfirst into horse ownership; the star became a frequent visitor to the Ben Howell & Son Saddlery in nearby Whitehaven, where he purchased a plethora of saddles and bridles, grooming items, and other necessities for the horses, along with riding apparel.

A pair of Elvis's riding boots from the King's Ransom Collection. *Photo courtesy Russ Howe Collection.*

While the existing stables and paddocks at Graceland could accommodate several horses, the structure was reportedly quite run down and in need of improvement. Elvis could have easily hired a crew to take on the project, but decided that he wanted the experience of making renovations himself. According to Schilling, "This was going to be a hands-on project. He'd be the carpenter. He'd be the painter. And, in the case of some extra buildings on the property that needed to be taken down to create a riding arena, he'd drive the bulldozer."[2] Allegedly, Elvis did not think the bulldozer his father had purchased was large enough, so he bought a bigger, more powerful machine and happily bulldozed several structures himself.

The quietness of the stable offered a new world of promise for Elvis. Working around the barn and caring for horses, he had found a way to relax and unwind, far away from the pressures of movie sets and the acting roles that were now unfulfilling to him. Elvis had discovered a sense of freedom and he began to enjoy every minute of it. The star's friend Marty Lacker would later recall, "Elvis would go out in the barn every day and every night. This barn had not been used in years. He fixed up a little office for himself and wrote the names of the horses on the stalls with a big red marking pen. He would write notes to himself, like 'What I'm Going To Buy Tomorrow' and 'What I'm Going To Do Tomorrow.' And he would clean up the barn and buy new tack. He just loved it."[3]

Elvis's office was on the second floor of his home, and the windows offered a splendid view of the horse pastures. Working in his office, as Elvis gazed through the windows, he could watch Priscilla and Sandy happily cantering their horses through the fields, their young faces radiating joy. The women frequently asked Elvis if he wanted to ride one of the horses, but he always politely declined until one day when he finally agreed to climb aboard Priscilla's horse, Domino. He simply loved it. "Now we all developed horse fever," Priscilla wrote in her memoir, *Elvis and Me.* "We rode late in the afternoons and well into the evenings."[4]

Most who knew Elvis have noted that when he enjoyed something, he always did it on a grand scale. He never did things half-heartedly, and the same applied to horses. "Elvis would go at everything in a big way," said his cousin, Billy Smith. "And when he got the horses, it was no different."[5] The star decided that his close friends should share in his passion, so they each received a horse. Then their wives or girlfriends received horses. Soon the stalls were brimming with equines of myriad colors and sizes, all of which were gifts from Elvis to his friends.

Despite concerns from Vernon Presley, who constantly worried about money, spending was of no real concern to Elvis. Dr. Edward Ogilve ("Doc") Franklin, the local veterinarian who cared for Elvis's horses, noted that Elvis sometimes overpaid for the horses he purchased. Doc Franklin remembered, "What Elvis did to the horse market

Elvis often wore a suede jacket such as this one while out riding his horses.
Photo courtesy of the Russ Howe Collection.

in northern Mississippi was unbelievable. We would go out and look at a horse that was a $300 horse, but when the people found out it was maybe for Elvis, it became a $3,000 horse."[6] Elvis, however, had no issue with spending freely as long as it made others happy. And he saw that his friends were thrilled with their horses, so the spending continued.

In the book, *Elvis Day by Day*, author Peter Guralnick reported that Elvis purchased several horses during the four-day span between December 28 and 31, 1966. These included a registered sorrel horse and a "yellow" horse (it was not specified whether this was a Buckskin or a Palomino), a chestnut horse called Whirlaway, a quarter horse gelding ("along with a large amount of tack"), a sorrel horse named Spurt, a bay horse named Guy, and an unnamed chestnut horse.[7] Adding to the tally of equines on the property, Colonel Parker sent some Shetland ponies to Elvis as a humorous gesture. According to friends, many of the guys enjoyed clowning around and, usually unsuccessfully, trying to ride the small, feisty ponies.

Dissatisfied with the direction of his career, Elvis had found happiness in caring for the horses. He had found something special in getting to know the soul of a horse. He spent hours in the barn, morning and night. According to sources, Elvis liked to keep the stable neatly organized, with all tack and supplies stored in their rightful places. Using a red felt-tipped pen, he noted the names of the horses and their riders on the walls. While Elvis would notate each individual person's name beside his tack, the superstar simply wrote, "Mine" under his own.

Alene Alexander, who began managing the Graceland stables after Elvis's death, said, "We just treasure that red Magic Marker writing in the tack room because if you know Elvis Presley's autograph, then you know that is his handwriting. He labeled places for ropes and the hackamores and all that stuff. And there's a note on the wall that says 'Don't move this TV.' That's in the tack room, too."[8]

Like so many others who love horses, Elvis Presley had discovered a world where he could simply be himself, leaving behind the overwhelming pressures of his mounting fame and stardom. If he felt sad or disappointed, a walk into the barn and the sound of contented horses would always make him smile. Armed with a newfound confidence and an ever-growing sense of peace, it was time for Elvis to find a horse of his own.

7

RISING SUN

By the end of 1966, Elvis had become quite the all-around horseman. Not only had he restored the barn and grounds at Graceland to accommodate his expanding herd of horses, but he had also overcome any earlier fears of riding that he may have harbored. Gifted with a naturally soft hand and seat, Elvis had become at ease in the saddle. As Elvis's comfort level increased, however, the quiet horse that he had selected as a possible mount was deemed a bit too mellow for his taste. Elvis thrived on excitement and challenge in all areas of his life; friends recall that he became easily bored. Eager for a more spirited animal, he passed the quiet horse along to a friend and began the search for a more suitable one.

While Elvis admired horses of all colors and breeds, his heart became set on owning a Palomino—a golden horse with a flowing white mane and tail. Palomino horses, which are designated as such by color rather than breed, have a long and illustrious history. According to legend, these golden steeds were revered by various kings and queens, most notably the Spanish Queen Isabella, who reportedly shipped Palominos to the newly discovered Americas. The longstanding choice of royalty, a Palomino would certainly befit the reigning king of rock and roll. Elvis was drawn to the Palomino not for its connection to royalty, but rather for its magnificent golden color. The singer thus set his sights on finding a suitable Palomino horse.

As is often reported in biographies, Elvis fought a life-long battle with insomnia that found him awake in the hours before dawn. In a way, this insomnia served its purpose; while most people were asleep, he could go outside without being mobbed by fans. It was during these early hours that Elvis would embark on his quest for a horse.

Accompanied by his friend Jerry Schilling, Elvis drove through rural farm areas at three and four o'clock in the morning, stopping at various farmhouses and knocking on strangers' doors. In the event that a weary farmer would answer, he would be surprised to see none other than Elvis Presley standing there. Once the farmer realized that he was not dreaming, the always polite, well-dressed Elvis would break the silence. "Hello, Sir. I am Elvis Presley," he would drawl, adding hopefully, "Do you have a golden Palomino for sale?"

The first few visits yielded no return; none of the stables had the horse that Elvis wanted. Soon, however, word of Presley's early morning farm visits made its way through the rural grapevine. It was then that Robert Boyd, a local breeder of Quarter Horses, heard of Presley's plight. Boyd had a horse that he thought would fit the bill.

"Midget's Vandy" was a four-year-old Quarter Horse gelding who stood a little over sixteen hands, with the rounded barrel and strong legs characteristic of his breed. In addition to his shiny golden coat, he had an attractive white-blazed face and three ivory stockings. The horse was flashy and well-trained, having carried Boyd's young daughter to numerous wins in local equestrian events. According to Boyd, he could also be a safe and willing mount for a less confident rider.

Convinced that this horse was exactly what Elvis wanted, Boyd approached Jerry Schilling. Boyd had come equipped with photos of the Palomino, including one that showed his daughter happily perched atop the horse, blue ribbons in hand. Schilling agreed to pass along the information to Elvis, who was not at home at the time.

When Schilling described Boyd's visit to Elvis, the singer was eager to see the horse. Upon arriving at Boyd's farm, Elvis took one look at the beautiful animal and purchased him on the spot. The cost was $3,000—a considerable sum at that time. Elvis immediately rechristened the horse "Rising Sun," or "Sun" for short. (Elvis was allegedly a fan of the song, "House of the Rising Sun," which had been recorded by Bob Dylan and later made popular by the Animals. While Elvis never recorded a studio version of the song himself, some have said that he did perform it at least once in concert.)

Shirley Connell, who was Elvis's neighbor for many years and penned the book, *Elvis: The Man in My Backyard*, remembers the fateful day when Rising Sun arrived at Graceland. Connell watched with anticipation as the horse trailer ambled up the long driveway and the hatch was opened to reveal a stunning, majestic Palomino. "I remember when Sun arrived. I looked at this drop-dead gorgeous palomino and was thinking, 'Now *that* is the horse for Elvis!'"[1]

Elvis and his Palomino, Rising Sun, shared a special bond. Here they are shown exploring the grounds of Elvis's home, Graceland, in early 1968. *Photo by Judy Palmer Bendewald.*

Elvis and Sun soon became constant companions. The horse was docile enough to further boost Elvis's level of confidence in the saddle, but had enough spunk to retain the singer's attention. Elvis rode him in a Western saddle, with the superstar looking every inch the cowboy in his matching hat and leather chaps. Together the pair galloped through the sprawling Graceland acreage, Elvis smiling widely as Sun loped effortlessly around the estate.

Often, Elvis gave his fans a special thrill by walking Sun down to the gates of Graceland and greeting those who waited outside. Video footage shows a glowing Elvis, happily chatting with folks and signing autographs while astride his gallant horse. These impromptu "autograph sessions" would sometimes last hours, demonstrating just how patient and kind Elvis was with his fans. Sun was sometimes not quite as patient, expressing his displeasure by tossing his head and flipping back his ears as his master signed an endless string of autographs. Finally, Elvis would bid his fans adieu and, to the delight of his audience, gallop Sun in a straight line in front of the crowd and back towards the barn. Shirley Connell notes that Elvis was careful about his fans' safety when around the horses. He would warn fans that unknowingly got too close to the horse's hindquarters that they should not stand near his back end in the event the horse was to kick.

Elvis donned cowboy attire while aboard Rising Sun in this undated photograph from the late 1960s. *Photo from the Russ Howe Collection.*

Like any true horseman, Elvis would often retreat to the quietude of the barn, where he spent hours brushing and talking (and sometimes singing) to his horse. He enjoyed grooming the horse's sleek golden coat and combing his silky white mane and tail. Elvis also cleaned and polished his own tack—which included the saddle, bridle, and bit—until it shined. When he rode, Elvis made sure to cool the horse out properly. Friends recall that he often took this to extremes, walking the horse for an hour when he had ridden for a mere fifteen minutes.

In his horse's honor, Elvis named the Graceland Stable "House of Rising Sun" and carefully painted those words above the stable doors. He also had the horse's name and likeness painted on the side of his white pickup truck. Elvis commissioned jeweler Sol Schwartz, of Schwartz & Ableser Jewelers of Beverly Hills, to create a special gold and diamond ring that featured a likeness of Rising Sun. The fourteen-karat gold ring included a horseshoe containing eighteen diamonds, with two additional diamonds as the horse's eyes.[2] The magnificence of the ring was a testament to Elvis's love and admiration for his horse.

As it provided him relief from the media's constant intrusion on his every move, Elvis's time spent with Sun was invaluable. In the years that followed, Rising Sun remained an important part of Elvis's life. It is safe to say that the golden horse was Elvis's "horse of a lifetime," bringing comfort to a man in desperate need of privacy. Sitting proudly on his horse's back, Elvis was able to experience true freedom. Friends recall how the singer would often saddle up in the early morning and ride off on his own in quiet solitude.

A radiant Elvis, aboard his favorite horse, Rising Sun, enjoyed mingling with the fans that gathered at Graceland to watch him ride. *Photo by Judy Palmer Bendewald.*

Priscilla Presley also recalled, "I remember one day I happened to look out of the window. It was twilight. The sky was aglow in misty blue and radiant pink. There was Elvis walking Rising Sun, his Golden Palomino. I saw them as silhouettes against the darkening sky. Elvis was walking slowly. I could practically hear him breathe. His breath was easy, his body relaxed. At that moment I was convinced that my husband had actually found peace."[3]

8

A NEW BEGINNING

On a cool winter morning in February 1967, as night was being transformed into day, Elvis was cruising along a country road in Horn Lake, Mississippi, approximately ten miles south of Graceland. Bundled inside an old pickup truck, Elvis and four friends—Priscilla, Jerry Schilling, Sandy Kawelo, and Alan Fortas—were headed for a local horse farm where Elvis hoped to find a Tennessee Walker for his father, Vernon. Alan steered the truck down the darkened road with Elvis sitting in the front seat.

Elvis soon noticed a cross that glimmered like a beacon at dawn, illuminating the surrounding emerald grass. The sight of an ivory concrete structure measuring fifty-five feet in height stopped Elvis in his tracks. It was approaching daybreak, and the sheer whiteness of this towering cross lit up the nearby field and trees.

Mesmerized, Elvis asked Alan to stop the truck in front of the property. "The way he told it," said his cousin, Billy Smith, "He just stood there a few minutes without saying anything. Then he said, 'This is the most beautiful sight. It

This towering white cross at "Twinkletown Farms" immediately caught Elvis's eye while the star was out driving on an early morning horse-buying trip in February 1967. *Photo courtesy of Whitney Lee.*

is so peaceful. I think it's a good omen.'"[1] Elvis looked on in wonder at the beauty that stood before him; there were acres upon acres of pristine land, sprinkled with handsome trees, grassy knolls, and rolling hills. In the center was a huge lake. A bridge, painted white just like the cross, spanned its length. The sun was beginning to rise, and its rays touched upon the expansive lake, shining like crystal confetti along the water. Near the front of the property was a charming little farmhouse surrounded by white concrete pillars. At the top of the property stood a "For Sale" sign.

This little cosmos that Elvis had discovered was known at that time as Twinkletown Farms. It belonged to a man by the name of Jack Adams, who had been an airline pilot for Chicago and Southern Airlines (later to be known as Delta). By 1966 Adams had retired from flying, and operated a lucrative business selling used aircraft out of nearby Twinkletown Airport.

In his spare time, Adams enjoyed farming and raising cattle at the sprawling ranch. He had spent a considerable amount of time enhancing the land in the years leading up to 1967. "It was a beautiful piece of property," Adams later recalled. "There was a little country home that I had remodeled and redone. It had a pretty good lake (that I had built) and a bridge across the lake and a great big cross sat right on the south side of the lake. It had 150 head of Santa

One of the features of the Circle G Ranch was an expansive lake that was filled with trout by then-owner Jack Adams prior to the ranch's purchase by Elvis. *Photo courtesy of Whitney Lee.*

Gertrudis cattle, too. We had a lot of people there and a lot of fun. That little lake was fresh and clean; I had a 10-inch well that pumped water into it, and I had it stocked with trout. It was a beautiful place."[2]

While Adams described the lake as "little," it was in fact immense, spanning ten to fourteen acres in diameter at that time. Over the shallowest part of the lake, Adams had erected a white footbridge that measured approximately 300 feet and was illuminated at night, much like the cross. The cross itself was surrounded by trees in a grassy knoll, and was situated approximately one hundred feet from where the lake ended.

Over the years there have been conflicting stories surrounding the origin of the cross. Some believe that it was built as a memorial to a lost relative, while others assert that it served as a beacon for nearby airplanes. However, Adams, a religious man, explained that it was purely a spiritual gesture. "God told me to build it," he later recalled. "[The cross] was well constructed. It was really pretty to see. I had a gentleman build it in Memphis. They hauled it down here and set it up so it was free-standing."[3] That cross served its purpose, and Elvis, being a spiritual man, instantly responded to it.

In fact, Elvis connected so strongly with the cross and the surrounding property that he decided to make an immediate offer to purchase Twinkletown Farms. At Elvis's urging, Alan Fortas spoke with Adams about purchasing the property and did so without mentioning his famous friend's name. The price, Fortas discovered, was $437,000—which included the aforementioned San Gertrudis cattle that were living on site at the time. Elvis agreed to purchase the ranch on the spot, with the condition that he could move in almost immediately, and left a down payment of $5,000 in the form of a check.

Decades later, in 1999, the check for the original down payment on the ranch, signed by Elvis as "E. A. Presley," was sold at auction for the sum of $7,680. The check, dated February 9, 1967, was written to Jack Adams and was drawn from an account with the National Bank of Commerce in Memphis, Tennessee. The check included a note that may have been made by Vernon Presley, which read: "As earnest money towards purchase of Twinkletown Farms, (160) acres all cattle equipment as stated in contract."

According to Jack Adams, the deal was finalized in a relatively simple transaction. "Elvis was a very, very fine, humble, pleasant, clean cut young man," Adams remembered. "He did exactly what he said he would do. He was really a nice gentleman."[4] In fact, Adams wanted to ensure that Elvis was making the right decision in purchasing the ranch, so he suggested that Elvis bring his friends and some of the horses over for a few days to gain a feel for the ranch life. Alan Fortas later recalled that Adams said, "Take all your people, use the house, ride the horses, and treat everything just as if it were yours."[5] Elvis packed up some belongings, loaded up some of the horses and tack, and rounded up his friends for a few days of ranch living.

Elvis's hairdresser and close friend, Larry Geller, remembers those days with great fondness. Geller recalls that the farmhouse at the ranch was a haven for various small treasures. Geller, an expert chess player, had taught Elvis's cousin Billy Smith the rules of the game, and the two men enjoyed playing it on a frequent basis. When Geller discovered an antique chess set in the house at Twinkletown Farms, he brought the set to Elvis's attention. According to Geller, Elvis enthusiastically gave him the set, stating, "Take it! I am buying the whole place!"[6]

Once the purchase and sales documents were signed and sealed, the proud new owner chose to rename the farm the Circle G Ranch. (Due to a registration issue, it was formally christened the Flying Circle G, but was always referred to simply as the Circle G.) There has been much speculation over the years as to whether the "G" stood for "Graceland"—as many say—or perhaps for Elvis's beloved mother, Gladys, but there has been no definitive answer. Elvis's friend George Klein recalled, "When the idea of naming the place was raised, Alan came up with the Circle G, and Elvis started to object, thinking the G was for Graceland. But when Alan explained that he was thinking of G for Elvis's mother, Gladys, the name took."[7]

While we may never know the true derivation of the ranch's name, we do know that the Circle G held special meaning for Elvis. As author Jerry Apps accurately surmised, "There were at least three 'G's' in [Elvis's] life: Gladys, Graceland, and God."[8]

Most importantly, the ranch brought a newfound sense of contentment to Elvis Presley. Many of his friends noticed a change in Elvis; he was no longer stressed or anxious and seemed happier and more content than he had been in the past. Ray Walker of the Jordanaires, who sang backup for Elvis and was a close friend, remembered, "The happiest we ever saw Elvis was when he first bought that ranch."[9]

As soon as the papers were signed, plans were made to permanently move the equines—including Elvis's beloved Rising Sun—from Graceland to their new home at the Circle G. Elvis had big plans for his new kingdom, and of course those plans included his beloved horses.

HOME AT THE CIRCLE G

The purchase of the Circle G provided a mounting sense of peace for Elvis—a serenity for which he had been searching for many years. Away from the pressures of Hollywood, the demands of Colonel Parker, and incessant media scrutiny, Elvis was able to immerse himself in the quietude of nature. The ranch, with its abundant landscape of hills, meadows, and water, offered Elvis a place of his own where he could enjoy a simpler life without the burdens that came with stardom.

"Elvis fell in love with the ranch," remembered his close friend Larry Geller. "He was searching for meaning outside of being 'Elvis Presley.' He was looking for grounding and searching for his identity as a human being—and his career simply did not fill that hole."[1]

Elvis committed himself, heart and soul, to creating a quiet utopia at the ranch. Shedding his superstar image, Elvis was happiest when working the land, tending to his horses, and enjoying the humble beauty of nature. "He no longer looked like a famous singer and movie star," remembered Elvis's friend Joe Esposito. "Wearing a cowboy hat and sheepskin jacket and sitting tall in the saddle, he was a dead ringer for the Marlboro man."[2]

In addition to its tranquil appeal, the massive land at the ranch offered seclusion that was not afforded at Graceland. As his herd expanded, Elvis realized that fourteen acres were not enough to accommodate so many horses. Safety also became an issue, as numerous people—most of whom were novice riders just learning to steer a horse—were cantering or galloping their horses in the same place at the same time. In fact, Elvis experienced firsthand the dangers created by this lack of space when his friend Red West inadvertently ran him down during a game of mounted cowboys and Indians.[3]

The safety aspect notwithstanding, the bustling shopping areas built on the land behind Graceland were encroaching on the privacy that Elvis desired. The much

A man and his horse. Elvis and Bear pose stylishly for the camera in this photograph taken at the Circle G Ranch in 1967. *Photo from the Russ Howe Collection.*

Modern-day view of the porch at the ranch house at Elvis's Circle G Ranch in Horn Lake, Mississippi. *Photo courtesy of Whitney Lee.*

larger, idyllic grounds of the Circle G fit the bill as a secluded hideaway for Elvis and his friends. "The back of Graceland had only so much land," Larry Geller explained. "We were all riding every day, and going as fast as we could. Elvis realized we needed more space."[4]

At home on the ranch, Elvis seemed to be happier and more content than ever. Geller paints a picture of his friend, energized and full of hope, sitting at the kitchen table at his Graceland home. The star was sketching feverishly, creating illustrations that would ultimately evolve into the logo for the Circle G Ranch. The final logo would consist of a circle with the letter "G" enveloped by wings on either side.

Once his drawing was complete, Elvis had his logo, or brand, applied to trucks, horse blankets, signs, and various other items at the ranch. In fact, there were many new items on which to affix the logo. Aside from tractors and other farm equipment, Elvis had decided that everyone at the ranch should have his own pickup truck. He began purchasing vehicles for his friends, ranch workers, and horse handlers, much to the dismay of his ever cost-conscious father, Vernon.

Elvis's extreme generosity, which has since become well-known, was in full swing at this time. When he found that there was an extra truck on hand, the star gave it to one of the workers who had been laboring at the ranch installing trailers. "I saw him ask one worker for a dollar," his life-long friend George Klein later recalled. "When the startled guy reluctantly handed him a crumpled bill, Elvis tossed him the keys to a Ford truck."[5]

Elvis's generous spending habits continued to trouble Vernon, who retained the bitter taste of poverty he had experienced as a younger man. But when the elder Presley questioned his son's penchant for spending, Elvis simply replied, "I'm having fun, Daddy, for the first time in ages. I've got a hobby that I look forward to getting up in the morning for."[6]

Elvis enjoyed the tranquility offered by the ranch, but he also liked being surrounded by his inner circle of friends, who often acted as personal bodyguards and were coined by the media as the "Memphis Mafia." A person who did not enjoy being alone, Elvis was most comfortable when surrounded by friends and family. In order to ensure that his friends could be at the ranch on a constant basis, he developed a plan to create a miniature community within the confines of the Circle G. The quickest way to do so, he surmised, was to purchase eight house trailers, which would be installed in a circle beneath a hilly spot near the lake area. Each house would be equipped with the proper electrical and plumbing amenities, and a septic system was constructed on the land. Additionally, after the public began crowding around the ranch, Elvis had a ten-foot-high wall built around the main parts of the property. While the work was performed by skilled laborers, all of it was planned and overseen by Elvis himself.

Vernon Presley proudly displays two fish that he caught in the lake at the Circle G Ranch in 1967. Note the white wooden cross in the background. *Photo from the Russ Howe Collection.*

"Elvis cast himself in the role of ranch foreman," Joe Esposito later said. "Every morning he saddled Rising Sun and rode out to issue instructions to the contractor on how to do things and where everything should go."[7]

Several of Elvis's closest friends received house trailers at the ranch, including the Schillings, the Espositos, the Gellers, and the Smiths, among others. Elvis and Priscilla originally moved into the brick ranch house. Soon afterwards, however, Elvis decided that he wanted to be a part of the miniature village he had created; he thus ordered a two-bedroom house trailer for Priscilla and himself, to be located in close proximity to the others.

It was a time of great togetherness for Elvis and his friends. In addition to riding horses, they enjoyed potluck suppers, barbecues, and various games. When it snowed, they would ride around the vast property on tractors and sleds, and playful snowball fights often ensued. In the spring, they witnessed the miracle of birth when several new calves and foals were born. Elvis was closer to nature than he had ever been, and he was enjoying it wholeheartedly. The star's happiness was reflected in his appearance and demeanor. According to some friends, at one point Elvis even let his hair go back to its natural sandy blond color.

"In becoming a ranch owner and turning the Memphis Mafia into a bunch of ranch hands," said George Klein, "Elvis had given himself a tremendous challenge, which he threw himself into fully. Making plans for the ranch, Elvis seemed more energetic and in charge than he had [been] in a long time—and that rubbed off on all of us."[8]

10

A PASSION FOR HORSES

When Elvis developed an interest in something, he did so on a grand scale. Horses, it seems, were no exception. Frustrated by the direction of his career, Elvis had found a true passion and was enjoying every moment to the fullest.

Through the winter of 1966–67, Elvis continued to buy equines of all colors, sizes, and breeds. Receipts from January of 1967 reveal that Elvis's purchases included a black mare and a buckskin mare, a horse called Keno for his friend Red West, an unnamed bay mare, a white buckskin, and a nondescript Quarter Horse called Conchita's Gold. Weeks later, he would add a "red chestnut" gelding and a Palomino mare to his herd. "He just kept buying more and

Larry Geller rides his horse Pokey Dunit, with Elvis and Rising Sun in the background, in this rare candid photo from 1967. *Photo courtesy of Larry Geller.*

more horses and more and more gear," said his friend George Klein.[1]

Larry Geller received a Texas-bred horse called Pokey Dunit, which provided much joy not only for him but also for his wife and two young children. The horse was brown, with a large, expressive, white star on its forehead. "Elvis wanted all of us to have a horse," he said. "And this horse was perfect for me. Even the kids would ride him and really enjoy it." Of course, they would need tack and riding apparel as well. "One day, Elvis called us into the tack room," Geller remembers. "And then he brought us all to a tack store, where we all got riding gear. It was fantastic. Elvis was so happy."[2]

Even those who did not want a horse, like George Klein and Alan Fortas, could not resist Elvis's sheer enthusiasm. Klein explained in his memoir that he never had much affection for horses, but Elvis's passion was so contagious that even he got in the saddle a few times. Alan Fortas recalled, "The Memphis Mafia were unlikely cowboys, but in Elvis' opinion, I had to have a horse." Fortas was unimpressed with the horse that Elvis had initially chosen for him, stating, "Elvis, it looks like a mule. I want one like Rising Sun, a Palomino."[3]

Ever the people pleaser, Elvis scoured the sale ads and finally found a Palomino called Model for his friend. Things did not go off without a hitch, however; Model kicked Rising Sun in the knee, resulting in a large, painful lump for Sun and an equally large vet bill for Elvis. From then on, Fortas remembered, Elvis kept Sun a good distance away from the other horses.

Regular vet care for Elvis's horses, both on a routine basis and for emergencies such as the injury to Sun's leg, was performed by Doc Franklin. Born and raised in Memphis, Doc Franklin would not only be a key member of Elvis's stable team, but also a close friend to the star for many years. He had attended the University of Tennessee Knoxville for pre-veterinary studies and graduated from Auburn University Veterinary School of medicine. After serving as a captain in the U.S. Army and obtaining a law degree, Dr. Franklin practiced veterinary medicine at Raines Road Animal Clinic in Whitehaven and DeSoto County Animal Clinic in Southaven, and tended to Elvis's horses for many years. (In 1987, Franklin would originate the "Images of the King" International Elvis Impersonator Contest, which is held annually in Memphis during Elvis Week as a tribute to his friend.)

Elvis would also enjoy hanging around the barn when his longtime farrier, Lim Couch, came to shoe the horses. Having graduated from farrier school in 1966, Couch began working for Elvis the following year and would remain in that role for the remainder of his lifetime. In interviews, Couch recalled that Elvis would come down to the barn and chat for hours while the farrier tended to Sun and the other horses. Couch, who was later inducted into the National Horseshoeing Hall of Fame, also remembered card games in the tack room, and noted that Elvis would sometimes stop by for a visit to the farrier's nearby barn.

A view of the barn area at the Circle G Ranch, which fell into disrepair in the decades following Elvis's death. The property is currently undergoing a restoration. *Photo courtesy of Whitney Lee.*

Like the other members of Elvis's stable team, Couch forged a lifelong friendship with the King.

Elvis spared no expense when it came to those he loved, including his horses. In addition to vet and farrier care, records show that he spent thousands of dollars at a time for various horse-related services and equipment. Many of these services were provided by "Mr. Bill" Spence of Graceland

Vernon and two of his stepsons (from his marriage to Dee Stanley) are shown with a mare and foal at Elvis's Circle G Ranch in 1967. *Photo from the Russ Howe Collection.*

Farms. Such services may have included basic horse training, as well as supplies such as bridles and blankets.

Elvis also purchased hay, grain, and salt blocks from Spence during this time. A weekly ledger made by Vernon Presley in January 1967 shows receipts for one hundred bales of hay totaling $135, twenty bags of horse feed at a total cost of $38, and ten blocks of salt at a total of $3. In order to transport the horses, at least one horse trailer was purchased from "Morris White" for a sum of $1,000.

Spence's son, Bill, who had been a classmate of Elvis's at Humes High School, was also helpful to the Presley stables at this time. The younger Spence sold saddlery and Western wear and served as the proprietor of Spence's Horse Service and Ranch Store on Millbranch Road in Memphis. Receipts show that Elvis purchased over $1,000 worth of "saddles and equipment for horses" in early 1967 from the younger Spence.

Many of Elvis's horses were purchased from the Spence farm as well. It appears that Spence may have allowed Elvis to take certain horses on a "trial" basis; records show that some were returned for credit, as they may have proven to be unsuitable for their riders, or, as was the case with one listed on the receipt, were unsound. Most of the horses purchased from Spence ranged in price from 250 to 750 dollars, while horses purchased from private owners—such as Elvis's Palomino, Rising Sun—cost several thousand dollars.

Colonel Midnight, Vernon's horse, was also purchased from the Spence family farm. Elvis had wanted to find an extra special horse for his dad—a black Tennessee Walker, a breed celebrated for its flashy movement and unique four-beat running-walk. Tennessee Walkers were originally bred in the southern United States, where their gaits proved useful on farms and plantations.

According to local lore, Colonel Midnight was owned by Bill Spence's wife, who was a bit reluctant to part with the horse until Elvis offered a hefty price. Despite the horse's bouncy gaits, Vernon developed a quick affinity for the horse and enjoyed riding him frequently. Originally simply called "Midnight," the horse had its name later lengthened to "Colonel Midnight" in homage to Elvis's manager, Colonel Tom Parker. Video footage shows a beaming Vernon Presley sitting proudly in the saddle as he steers Colonel Midnight through the grounds of Graceland.

Another addition to Elvis's string of horses around this time was a bay, grade mare known as Ingram. A fan of word puns, Elvis jokingly renamed the horse "Mare Ingram" in honor of William B. Ingram, mayor of Memphis, who was lobbying at that time to change the name of the "Mid-South Coliseum" to "Elvis Presley Coliseum." (Unfortunately, Ingram's efforts were overruled by the city officials, who stated that a building could not be named after a living person.)

"There were so many horses that even just naming them became a challenge," said George Klein. "Though

Elvis did have some fun with that."[4] Other horses that Elvis affixed with symbolic names included Big Red, named for Elvis's friend Red West; Flaming Star, after Elvis's film of the same name; Beauty, named for a horse in the James Dean film *Giant*; and Buckshot, named after one of Wild Bill Hickok's horses.

Perhaps the most significant of all of Elvis's horse purchases, besides Rising Sun, was an "American bred saddle horse" that cost $5,000 and was purchased from Alfred Page, according to a ledger entry made by Vernon. While there is no documentation of this horse's name or other distinguishing characteristics, the ledger entry most likely refers to Bear, a beautiful black gaited horse that was among Elvis's favorites to ride. There is no detailed information regarding Bear's lineage or registered name, but it is likely, from photographic evidence, that he was a Tennessee Walker. He had large, kind, wide-set eyes and the shape characteristic of Walking Horses. "Bear was a gorgeous horse," Larry Geller remembers, noting the tall gelding's even, rhythmic gaits. "Elvis said that horse was as smooth as a Cadillac."[5]

Elvis had originally fallen in love with Tennessee Walking Horses when visiting the Lennox Farm in Collierstown, Tennessee, a ranch owned by millionaire George L. Lennox. A businessman by trade, Lennox was a noted breeder

Elvis is shown aboard his cherished Tennessee Walker, Bear, in this undated photograph from the late 1960s. *Photo from the Russ Howe Collection.*

of Walking Horses, and stood the 1964 grand champion stallion, Carbon Copy, at his farm. Priscilla remembered that she, Elvis, and Alan Fortas had visited the Lennox farm when looking for a horse for Vernon.

"The owner was George L. Lennox and he showed Elvis his pride and joy—Grand Champion Carbon Copy," Priscilla wrote. "Elvis thought it was the most beautiful horse he'd ever seen. Then George asked if he'd like to see how he rode. Well that was it…Elvis wanted a Tennessee Walking horse. So he purchased Bear."[6]

With all of the horses now relocated from Graceland to the Circle G, Elvis had 160 acres on which to ride and explore new surroundings. He became more and more self-assured in the saddle, displaying little, if any, of the fear he had experienced after the mishap incurred during *Flaming Star*. On at least one occasion, Elvis piloted Sun across the narrow, snow-covered footbridge over the lake during winter, which demonstrated the complete trust that existed between horse and rider. A sign that currently stands at the bridge reads: "Bridge erected as a shortcut across the lake. Elvis crossed it once riding 'Sun' while it was covered with snow and ice. It was always lighted."

Bolstered by excitement for the ranch and all it had to offer, Elvis would get up early in the morning—which was unusual for him, as he was notorious for sleeping during

View of the footbridge crossing the lake at the Circle G Ranch. Elvis rode across this bridge on Rising Sun on a winter's day in 1967. *Photo courtesy of Whitney Lee.*

the daytime and staying up all night. After breakfast, he would tack up Rising Sun and ride for hours, exploring the fields, meadows, and trails of the Circle G. Often he would bring along a package of bread or rolls to serve as sustenance if he became hungry while riding, securing the package to the saddle by twisting it around the front of the horn. According to Priscilla, "It wasn't unusual to see him walking across the property, knocking on doors, waking everyone up, or checking on the horses in the early morning hours. He was having a ball."[7] In fact, Elvis was having so much fun that, for the first time in his career, he did not want to return to making films.

Elvis had been scheduled by Colonel Parker in February to begin recording songs for the upcoming film *Clambake*. The movie was to be yet another "formula film" for Elvis, following the corny, shallow plotlines that the star had grown to despise. Understandably, Elvis did not want to leave behind the beauty and tranquility of his ranch and return to what he sometimes considered the superficial world of Hollywood. As the deadline approached in mid-February, Elvis was able to convince Colonel Parker to hold the recording sessions for the film in Nashville rather than Hollywood.

At this time in his life, Elvis had a fear of flying that had been fueled by a terrifying experience on a flight to Nashville in early 1956, in which the plane encountered engine trouble and was forced to make an emergency landing. Elvis's mother, Gladys, had also worried about her only child traveling by plane, which likely fueled his fears. Whenever possible, Elvis would avoid flying, traveling instead by car, bus, or train. However, as Larry Geller recalls, Elvis was quite content at the ranch and had put off leaving for Nashville. He delayed the trip for so long that he was about to be late. Ever the professional, and with time being of the essence, Elvis decided to ask his neighbor, Kemmons Wilson, if he would fly the group to Nashville on his private jet. Wilson, the founder of the Holiday Inn chain of hotels, heartily agreed to help his neighbor out.[8]

On February 23, Elvis and his entourage traveled by plane to the recording studio in Nashville to record some of the preliminary tracks for *Clambake*. Perhaps not wishing to fully leave behind the pleasures offered by the ranch, Elvis arrived at the studio wearing a complete cowboy outfit, including a hat and chaps. During the time Elvis was in Nashville, construction continued at the Circle G, including the installation of a quarter mile of temporary fencing.

Upon his return to the ranch, Elvis continued to ride his horses every day, so much so that he developed painful saddle sores. Riders often develop these blisters and raw patches of skin when their legs rub against the leather of the saddle, and the pain can be agonizing. As Elvis's physician was not available to examine him on that Sunday afternoon, Charlie Hodge arranged for him to be seen by Memphis physician Dr. George Nichopoulos (commonly referred to as "Dr. Nick"), with whom Hodge was acquainted. Given the painful nature of Elvis's condition, the physician agreed to make a house call to the ranch rather than asking the singer to make the trip into Memphis. Nichopoulos would remain Elvis's personal physician for the remainder of the singer's life.

After examining Elvis's injuries and prescribing some topical medication, the doctor packed his bag to return to his office in Memphis. As he was leaving, Elvis expressed concern that he would not be well enough to begin work on *Clambake* that week as expected. "Elvis explained that the cast and crew were in Hollywood ready to shoot his new movie, and he had decided his saddle sores were still too painful for him to travel," the doctor later said. "He knew it would be expensive if he did not show up on time. He thought the Colonel needed to be informed so he could utilize the two days for some other aspect of the movie."[9] Elvis preferred that the doctor convey this request to the Colonel directly, and, dialing the telephone, handed the receiver to Nichopoulos. After speaking with the doctor, the Colonel agreed to request a second postponement for *Clambake* with United Artists. Filming would be delayed until the first week in March.

As Nichopoulos was exiting the gates of the ranch, one of the guys called him back; Elvis wished to convey his gratitude by giving the doctor a full tour of the ranch. "We climbed into a heavy-duty, dusty, white pickup and Elvis drove us over a good part of his 163 acres of beautiful, rolling fields. We had a nice visit. I found Elvis to be a naturally warm person and an interesting conversational-ist," Nichopoulos later wrote. "Charlie [Hodge] later told me that Elvis had bought all the trucks and house trailers I had seen for his guys—as well as the horses and western outfits—the whole deal."[10]

As he drove away, Dr. Nichopoulos could understand why Elvis was reluctant to return to Hollywood. "He had created this insular world in an attempt to enjoy a normal life," the doctor said. "In all the years that followed," he added, "I would never again see Elvis look as relaxed as he did that day."[11]

11

RETURN TO REALITY

By early March 1967, with two postponements granted on the film *Clambake*, it was time for Elvis to leave behind the confines of the Circle G ranch. On March 5, Elvis and his entourage traveled to Los Angeles to begin work on the movie—another in a string of bland musical comedies with weak plotlines and subpar songs. Filming would be further delayed due to some minor production difficulties, and again when Elvis accidentally slipped in the bathroom and hit his head on the tub, suffering a minor concussion. Given such delays, principal filming for the movie would ultimately begin on March 20; there are reports that Elvis was able to return, albeit briefly, to the Circle G before filming.

The ranch had to be a welcome respite for Elvis, who was roundly uninterested in working on this film. Jerry Schilling wrote that *Clambake* "had every indication of being his lousiest production yet. I know it just bothered the hell out of him—his music was being messed with, his once-promising film career had been turned into a joke, and he didn't see any way out. The idea of turning a ranch into a refuge for himself had to be appealing."[1] Despite his feelings, Elvis, who was always the consummate professional, returned to Hollywood to fulfill his obligations.

When filming on *Clambake* paused in early April, Elvis was able to return to the Circle G for a period of several weeks, during which he rode Rising Sun nearly every day. By now, construction at the ranch had been completed and Elvis was able to fully enjoy all of its amenities. As the ranch operations expanded, stable hands had been hired to help care for the horses. The primary manager of Elvis's stable was Mike McGregor, a veteran horseman and saddle maker whom Elvis had befriended during his many trips to the local tack shop. In order to provide full-time care for the horses, McGregor and his family lived on-site at the Circle G. A kindly man who usually donned a smile and a crisp cowboy hat, McGregor not only managed Elvis's growing stables, but also provided training and refreshing

Elvis poses aboard his beloved Tennessee Walking Horse, Bear, in this candid photograph taken on January 1, 1968. © *Magma Agency / WireImage /Getty Images.*

for the various horses at the ranch. McGregor was an accomplished rider who could entertain Elvis and his friends by performing tricks, including standing in the saddle while on the back of Rising Sun.

Bonding over their shared love of all things equine, Elvis and McGregor became close friends. "[Elvis] was the greatest guy in the world to work for," McGregor later recalled of the man he called "Boss." "Working for him was kind of like just doing something for a friend. He never even raised his voice to me."[2]

With Elvis's encouragement, McGregor enrolled in some night classes in metal smithing at the Memphis Art Academy and developed a penchant for creating fancy accents on saddles, concert belts, and other leatherwork. Together with his seamstress wife, Barbara, McGregor would create various costume accessories for Elvis in the years that followed, including the King's trademark "TCB" belts and jewelry. In later years, McGregor would own and operate a jewelry and leather business that served such well-known clients as Johnny Cash, Carl Perkins, Roy Orbison, and others.

As the stable manager, Mike McGregor was an essential member of Elvis's team for many years, particularly when the star was in Hollywood working on films and, later, when he was on tour. In late April 1967,

Elvis would also be away from home when he and Priscilla flew to Las Vegas for their wedding on May 1. Following the ceremony at the Aladdin Hotel, the couple
and their friends traveled to Palm Springs, California,
for a brief honeymoon. Elvis apparently missed his
horses, as he, Priscilla, and their friends went horseback
riding in the mountains while in Palm Springs, according
to his cousin Billy Smith.[3] It was then back to the Circle

Modern-day view of the "honeymoon cottage" at the Circle G Ranch, where
Elvis and Priscilla spent time during the early weeks of their marriage. *Photo
courtesy of Whitney Lee.*

G, where the newlywed couple continued their honeymoon at the ranch, likely staying in the more secluded brick farmhouse rather than in the house trailer. For this reason, the farmhouse at the Circle G was later dubbed "The Honeymoon Cottage."

During the following weeks, the group enjoyed riding their horses almost every day. On one occasion, as Elvis, Priscilla, and their friends galloped along the Circle G's vast acreage, Elvis lost his wedding ring. It was never to be found. Priscilla later recalled of the incident, "It was a little big on his ring finger. We were racing our horses Rising Sun and Domino at our Circle G Ranch. He raised his hand and pointed to head toward the house and it fell off his finger. It was impossible to find. I did give him another one that looked just like it."[4]

The idyllic times at the Circle G would soon come to a halt, as Hollywood came calling in the form of a film called *Speedway*. On June 10, Elvis and his entourage set out for California to begin work on this movie that co-starred Nancy Sinatra, daughter of the famed crooner Frank Sinatra. While the film was yet another formulaic musical comedy that lacked substance, Elvis made the most of the experience. He got along well with the younger Sinatra, just as he had enjoyed working with her father, years before, on a TV special that welcomed him back from the Army.

Elvis's spirits were further lifted during the filming of this movie when he announced that Priscilla was expecting the couple's first child.

Following the completion of *Speedway*, Elvis would begin work on a Western-themed comedy called *Stay Away, Joe*. On August 21, Elvis began makeup tests for his role as rodeo rider Joe Lightcloud, a Navajo who attempts to save his family's reservation by developing a lucrative cattle business. After completion of the makeup tests on August 26, Elvis was able to return to the ranch.

In spite of his love for the Circle G, Elvis was facing mounting pressure from both his father and Colonel Parker to sell the ranch—for different reasons. Vernon was frantic that Elvis was about to go bankrupt from his spending on the ranch. Parker, on the other hand, did not like the idea of Elvis disappearing for hours at a time, where he was unable to reach the star to discuss business matters and could not keep Elvis under his strict control. As Elvis's schedule now allowed for little time to be spent at the Circle G, Vernon began to sell off various ranch items, including trucks, mobile homes, and cattle.

On October 8, 1967, Elvis traveled to scenic Sedona and Cottonwood, Arizona to begin work on *Stay Away, Joe*, with some scenes filmed at the historic Cottonwood Hotel. While he was in Arizona, Elvis purchased Western

In this publicity still from *Stay Away, Joe*, Elvis (as Joe Lightcloud) poses with his character's horse, "Old Grey." Later in the film, Joe trades his horse for a Cadillac automobile. *Photo courtesy of Photofest Inc.*

wear for himself at the hotel's Robinson Clothier Western Wear Store, indicating that he still had the ranch on his mind. Filming *Stay Away, Joe* must have frustrated Elvis immensely, as the movie included some rather absurd storylines. In the opening scene, Joe drives cattle at his family's reservation in a white Cadillac convertible; later, his friend accidentally barbecues a highly prized bull. Perhaps most humiliating of all, however, was a song that Elvis was forced to sing to Dominic, a stud bull that showed little interest in mating. Elvis was apparently so uncomfortable with this song that he asked producer Felton Jarvis to promise that it would never be released as a record.

Despite its mediocrity, *Stay Away, Joe* did call for Elvis's character to ride horseback. During several early scenes in the movie, the star was filmed riding bareback on a large, grey horse. In one such scene, Joe Lightcloud rides "Old Grey" to a used car dealership, where he trades the animal for a red convertible. Elvis appeared relaxed and at ease on horseback in this film, likely owing to his countless hours in the saddle at the ranch and his experience as a horse owner.

Well-known movie horse trainer Bobby Davenport and his friend, wrangler Joe Craigmile, served as the on-set horse trainers for *Stay Away, Joe*. During breaks from filming, the two men visited a local ranch, where they noticed a grulla mule romping in a field. Davenport purchased the mule on the spot and brought her to the movie set, where she was trained in how to perform on camera. *Stay Away, Joe* thus marked the film debut for Mousey the mule, who would go on to have a lengthy career in Hollywood. In addition to *Stay Away, Joe*, Mousey would appear in films starring John Wayne, among others, and in several TV series, including *Lassie*, *Quest*, and *Bret Maverick* (the latter starring James Garner).

Filming on *Stay Away, Joe* wrapped in mid-to-late November 1967. By this time, due to scheduling constraints, Elvis was hardly spending any time at the Circle G. Alan Fortas was assigned with the task of acting as ranch foreman, but it was difficult to maintain the ranch operations without Elvis on site. As a result, the horses were moved back to the stables at Graceland, and the ranch was offered for sale. On November 4, 1967, a public auction was held at the Circle G, which drew 2,000 fans and collectors. The sale, which included tractors and trailers, TVs and electronics, and various other items, collectively raised over $108,000.

Elvis was not ready to part with the ranch just yet, however. During the Christmas season, he and his entourage spent some quality time riding the horses that remained

at the ranch and that had not yet been trailered back to
Graceland. It was to be a bittersweet farewell to the sprawling property that had brought the star such pleasure and
freedom. The Circle G would ultimately be sold on May
20, 1969 for the sum of $440,000.

Despite the fact that Elvis had given up the Circle G
ranch, the King's love for and enjoyment of his horses
would never wane. Rising Sun, Bear, and the other horses
settled back into their stalls at Graceland, where Elvis continued to lovingly care for them and ride them whenever he
was at home. It was a love affair that would continue for
the remainder of his life.

12

KING OF HEARTS

As the holiday season passed and the last of the horses were moved from their stalls at the ranch, Elvis likely felt a tinge of disappointment. Fortunately, the promise of the new year dissolved any lingering sense of regret for the star, who was preparing for his most important role—fatherhood. On February 1, 1968, Elvis's only child, daughter Lisa Marie, was born in Memphis. Elvis was, by all accounts, a doting father who beamed with pride at the very mention of Lisa's name. When she was old enough, Lisa would have her own pony, a Shetland mare by the name of Moriah.

In the weeks before and after Lisa Marie's birth, Elvis spent much of his time at Graceland, during which he was often observed in the saddle aboard both Rising Sun and Bear. Judy Palmer Bendewald, a lifelong fan and author of the book *My Treasured Memories of Elvis*, photographed a cheerful Elvis riding Rising Sun on many occasions during these cool winter months. Bendewald recalls that Elvis and his "Memphis Mafia" friends rode horses down to the Graceland gates or along the fence on the south side of the lawn almost every day in early February of 1968. Usually dressed in a sporty leather jacket, with matching black

Elvis and Bear in action in the riding ring at Graceland in the late 1960s. *Photo from the Russ Howe Collection.*

gloves and chaps embossed with white trim, Elvis often conversed with Bendewald and her friends, as well as with other fans that had gathered at the end of the long driveway.

On one occasion, Bendewald snapped photos as Elvis was cantering Rising Sun accompanied by two members of his entourage: Charlie Hodge, who rode a sturdy chestnut, and Marvin "Gee Gee Gambill," who was aboard a yellow buckskin. Gee Gee was a member of the Presley family, having recently married Elvis's cousin Patsy, the daughter of Vernon's younger brother, Vester. A tall, greying man who bore a striking resemblance to his brother, Vester served as the gatekeeper at Graceland for many years. He often chatted with the young fans that were "regulars," providing them with soft drinks and allowing them to enter the gates as they waited for Elvis to appear.

On this particular day, as Vester was not working, Bendewald and the other fans remained outside the gates. At approximately 4:30 p.m., Elvis galloped Sun over the left (north) hill with his riding companions, which now also included Jerry Schilling. "They looked like the Rough Riders," Bendewald remembered. Noticing that Vester was not around, Elvis wanted to ensure that his regular fans were still allowed inside the gates and thus instructed the security guards to allow the girls to walk onto the property. "It's alright," Elvis said. "They can stand inside."[1]

Elvis and friends enjoyed riding on the sprawling grounds of Graceland in February 1968, often putting on a show for fans who lingered nearby. *Photo by Judy Palmer Bendewald.*

Within a few minutes, Bendewald recalls, there were over one hundred fans spilling inside the iron gates. "Elvis talked and signed autographs for about twenty minutes," she recalled. "Someone said, 'Look at what you've gotten yourself into.' Elvis replied, 'Yeah, I know.' Another fan said it looked like he was having fun and he said, 'You're right, baby.'"[2]

Bendewald presented Elvis with a personalized scrapbook, a gift from the singer's Australian Fan Club, and he happily posed for photographs as he held the book in his gloved hands. Bendewald noted that Rising Sun was resistant to standing still at this time, so Elvis had to maintain a firm hold on the reins in order to make him halt. Elvis held a small, thin cigar between his teeth as he posed for the photograph.

Snapshots and video footage taken of Elvis during this time reveal a gifted horseman with a secure, yet soft, seat and a gentle hand, even when his horse was pulling back on the reins, resisting contact. Elvis shows excellent posture in the saddle, with his legs lightly resting against the horse's sides. It appears that Elvis was quite a natural on horseback. The connection between horse and rider is evident even in the stillness of the aged photographs.

Elvis's willingness to share this private time with his fans reveals his kindness and depth of character. Few performers of his magnitude, then or now, would have taken the time to mingle with crowds when he was supposed to be enjoying quiet moments with his horses. Despite his worldwide fame, Elvis never forgot where he came from and he viewed himself as no different from any other person. He considered himself extremely fortunate to achieve

Elvis poses aboard Rising Sun on the Graceland lawn in February 1968. The star is holding a scrapbook that was a gift to him from the Australian fan club. *Photo by Judy Palmer Bendewald.*

all that he had, and was happy to share the horses he loved with his legions of loyal, steadfast fans.

Elvis loved his horses, and all animals, so much so that he ensured that they were always protected from harm. Larry Geller remembers an incident when a young, hotshot trainer was hired to assist with the animals. When one of the horses—a beautiful Appaloosa—began to rear up out of fear, the young man smacked the animal so violently that the horse lost its balance and fell to the ground. Elvis was so upset by this man's treatment of the horse that he not only told the trainer to never lay his hands upon any of his animals again, but also made sure that the man was immediately fired from his job at Graceland.[3]

Of course, Elvis's deep, fun-loving sense of humor also made its way into the stables, as he always enjoyed playing practical jokes on others. In a televised interview with Stina Dabrowski, Elvis's daughter Lisa remembered that her father once brought a pony into the house, much to the horror of his strict grandmother, Minnie May. Elvis also taught Rising Sun to drink Pepsi (the King's favorite drink) from a can and occasionally fed the horse sugar cookies as a treat.

Of all the stories surrounding Elvis and his love of horses, however, perhaps none is as poignant as the account told by author and friend to the King, Jim Curtin.

According to Curtin, Elvis had heard about a seven-year-old "horse crazy" girl named Kim Sparks, who lived in Walls, Mississippi, not far from the Circle G Ranch. Kim, like many young girls, longed and hoped for a horse of her own. Elvis had been told that little Kim went out to the ranch nearly every day, hoping for a glimpse of Elvis riding Rising Sun. Allegedly, the youngster would sit atop the fence surrounding the ranch and watch Elvis ride for hours at a time, mesmerized by the sight of the King aboard his beautiful golden Palomino. Curtin wrote:

> Elvis found out that it was Kim's birthday. He went over to her house and asked to see her. Mrs. Sparks called her daughter to the door, and Kim looked up at her visitor wide-eyed. Elvis crouched in front of her and told her that a friend of his had told him it was her birthday. Kim told him that it was. Elvis replied, "Good, because I don't know what I would do with your present if it wasn't." Kim looked at Elvis with apprehension and in a small, shaky voice, asked, "What present?" Elvis wrapped his big hand around her tiny one and led her to the trailer which contained her new horse. Kim began to cry. She ran to Elvis and hugged him as hard and as tight as she could.

She held onto Elvis for quite some time, and her sobs never ceased. Tears rolled down Elvis' face at the child's genuine appreciation of his gift. No one, young or old, had ever reacted to him quite that way before.[4]

According to Curtin, when Elvis told friends about Kim Sparks and her horse, even after many years had passed, his eyes were filled with tears of joy. "If one can't give what they have and share," he was known to say, "they will always be empty."

13

THE MAN CALLED CHARRO

In mid-July 1968, Elvis and his entourage traveled to Apache Junction, Arizona, to begin work on *Charro!*, which was to be the final Western film of his career. The word "charro," when translated from Spanish, refers to a "traditional horseman." In the opening scenes of the movie of the same name, Elvis appears every inch the rugged cowboy. With a beard (for the first and only time on film) and a wide-brimmed hat pulled slightly over his eyes, the King commands attention on screen as reformed outlaw Jess Wade. Elvis exudes poise and swagger in the saddle as he guides his chestnut horse through the winding mountains and valleys of the "old West."

Charro!, originally entitled *Come Hell, Come Sundown*, had been written as a vehicle for Western star Clint Eastwood. Due to a contract dispute with Paramount, however, Eastwood was not allowed to work with National General Pictures, forcing him to withdraw from the film. Following Eastwood's departure, many of the movie's financial backers followed suit. The result was a budget of only $1.5 million for the film, which was set to emulate the "spaghetti Westerns" that were popular at the time. (In contrast, the top grossing film of 1968, *2001: A Space Odyssey*, had a budget of $10.5 million.)

Charro! tells the story of gunfighter Wade, whose former gang members attempt to frame him for the theft of a jewel-encrusted Mexican cannon. In one scene, Wade is captured by his former band of outlaws, who proceed to brand his cheek with a blistering iron. Like most Westerns, the film includes various equine-based scenes, one of which involved roping and taming a wild stallion.

The equine scenes for the movie were filmed at the famed Apacheland Movie Ranch, which was set up to resemble an old Western town and allowed access to the public during production. Other scenes were filmed at Old Tucson Studios, which had been built in 1939 for the filming of the movie *Arizona* starring William Holden. In keeping with the spirit of the film, the star's entourage (and even Colonel Parker) decided to join Elvis and grow beards themselves. A bearded Jerry Schilling served as a stand-in for Elvis in certain scenes of the film.

Elvis's ease in the saddle is apparent in his onscreen portrayal of the confident Jess Wade, and was also evident during rehearsals. Alan Fortas noted that the horse Elvis was riding began to act up, but the King, by then an accomplished horseman, remained unfazed. "I brought my camera to the set," Fortas later recalled, "where I took some pictures of him looking confident on a rearing horse."[1] As he had done in other films, Elvis performed some of the basic riding scenes in *Charro!* himself.

In one such scene, a horseless Jess Wade lugs his saddle through the mountainous range, where he stumbles upon a herd of wild mustangs. Wade manages to rope a fractious black horse and later rides the animal, which proceeds to buck and rear for a period of several minutes. Some have assumed that Elvis performed the roping and taming stunts himself, and Elvis certainly had the skills in the saddle by this time to warrant such assumptions. However, given the insurance considerations and the possibility of the star becoming injured during filming, the studio used a trained stunt double for the most dangerous scenes.

By the time he filmed *Charro!*, Elvis was a skilled and confident rider. Friend
Alan Fortas recalled seeing Elvis atop this rearing horse on the set of the film.
Photo courtesy of Photofest Inc.

The more hazardous stunts involving horses were performed not by Elvis, but rather by Rodd Wolff, a professional stunt rider. Wolff, who was raised in Phoenix, began riding horses and practicing stunts at the tender age of eight years. Mentored by the legendary stuntman Jock Mahoney, Wolff became an accomplished horseman while still a teen. In addition to riding and roping, he earned fame as a trainer of falling horses in Westerns, war films, and other action-based movies, working primarily on those filmed in his home state. (Wolff was also originally hired as The Marlboro Man, but was released when the cigarette company discovered that he was a non-smoker.)

While Wolff completed the film's most hazardous stunts with horses, Elvis was required to perform in some of the close-up shots. For the roping scene, Elvis had to hold onto the rope as the horse fought valiantly against him, which resulted in the star sustaining painful burns on his hands.

Sandy and June Evans, two young fans who visited the *Charro!* set, recalled, "The last day Elvis filmed here, they were doing some scenes on location in a really wild canyon. The scene showed Elvis roping a big, black wild stallion which he rides in the picture. He is holding the rope and the horse is bucking and rearing and dragging him around. It's very exciting. After the first take, he kept looking at his

While stunt riders were used for the most challenging scenes of *Charro!*, Elvis had to perform the close-ups himself. This scene resulted in the star sustaining rope burns on his hands. *Photo courtesy of Photofest Inc.*

hands and rubbing them on the sides of his pants. By the time they had done the scene two more times, his hands were badly rope burned. That evening, after dinner, as he was leaving the hotel for another location, we spoke to him again and he had Band-Aids on his fingers and the palms of his hands. When he tried to sign some autographs, you could tell that it was an effort even to hold the pen. You know that he must have been in pain."[2]

True to his nature, Elvis did not allow such injuries to limit his interactions with fans. "Elvis came over to the roped off area to talk and sign autographs. He is so marvelous with his fans," Sandy and June told the media in 1968. "Elvis has a way of making each one feel important. When he talks to you, he gives you his undivided attention, in spite of everything that is going on around him."[3]

When *Charro!* was released to the public, it garnered less than stellar reviews. Despite the film's lack of praise, however, some critics realized that Elvis was not the one at fault for its mediocrity. "Don't blame the King for this bleak routine western being so stiff," wrote film critic Dennis Schwartz. "He tries his best; blame writer-director Charles Marquis Warren."[4]

14

A TRUE PERFORMER

While *Charro!* ultimately proved a disappointment for Elvis, the King's career was about to receive a much-needed boost. Prior to filming *Charro!*, he had been given an opportunity to resurrect his singing career, which many believed was on a downward swing. Tied to obligations in the movie world, Elvis had not performed in front of a live audience since 1961, and his last chart-topping single was released in 1962. While Elvis was away from live performing, British bands such as the Beatles had ascended to rock and roll's highest pinnacle.

Besides a decline in Elvis's popularity as a music star, his movies had been earning less money at the box office, leading Colonel Parker to seek out an alternate plan. The result was a deal with NBC to finance one movie (1969's *Change of Habit*) along with a televised special that would air during the 1968 holiday season. The latter, to be produced by the young director Steve Binder, would be filmed in front of a live audience. Binder had achieved success with music specials in the past, having directed the classic 1964 concert film *T.A.M.I. Show*, which featured the Rolling Stones, the Beach Boys, and James Brown, among others. The TV special, Binder surmised, would allow Elvis to reestablish his reputation as a musician and regain his rightful place as the king of rock and roll.

Elvis's NBC special was a tremendous success, earning him unanimous rave reviews. Broadcast on television on December 3, 1968, the special included an outstanding mixture of informal "jam" sessions and choreographed numbers, catapulting Elvis—dressed dashingly for much of the special in a black leather suit—back into the spotlight. Known informally as the "Comeback Special," Elvis's program was the highest-rated television special of the year, and, according to Binder, was likely the first one-man TV special to appear on commercial American television.

Elvis's "Comeback Special" not only brought the star tremendous acclaim, but also enabled him to return to his roots in live performing. Capitalizing on the success of the special, Colonel Parker negotiated a deal with Alex Shoofey of the International Hotel in Las Vegas, which was still under construction at that time. No longer tied down by ponderous movie contracts, Elvis began a stint in Las Vegas on July 31, 1969, where he performed for a sold-out crowd that included stars such as Pat Boone, Paul Anka, Fats Domino, and Dick Clark, among others. Elvis would eventually play more than 700 sell-out performances through 1976 at the International, which had, by that time, become the Las Vegas Hilton.

The King also made a triumphant return to the music charts, where he claimed the U.S. #1 spot with 1969's "Suspicious Minds" and followed that with a UK #1 hit, "The Wonder of You," in 1970. Later he would tour across the United States, where he dazzled the crowds with a string of sold-out concerts.

Interestingly, before returning to live performing, Elvis spent more time riding his horses in front of fans on the Graceland lawn. In the book, *Elvis Day By Day*, author Peter Guralnick wrote that, in the months leading up to his first concert in July 1969, Elvis would often ride his horses down to the gates and spend time with fans "in what appear[ed] to be a conscious strategy to renew his roots before going out in public again to perform."[1] Elvis's Uncle Vester noted that Colonel Parker was opposed to such activities, but Elvis felt that he needed "to get used to the crowds again." Elvis was no longer wearing cowboy attire while riding Sun, as he had in the days of the Circle G Ranch. Now the star was dressed in more formal clothing, such as white pants and a flowing red or purple blouse with a scarf. Given the high temperatures of the season, which could often exceed one hundred degrees, Elvis typically rode in the late afternoon so that the horses would not become overheated.

Gary Pepper, a disabled man who became a close personal friend of Elvis's, recalled that Elvis could often be seen during this time "riding the horses in the side lot and front grounds of Graceland putting on quite a show for everyone to see."[2] Pepper noted that many fans threw various objects over the stone wall for Elvis to sign as he was riding Sun near the front of the yard. Elvis graciously autographed the items and threw them back over the wall for the fans to retrieve.

According to Pepper's account, on another occasion, Elvis rode down near the gates to find that at least 500 fans had congregated. A traffic jam began on the highway as folks slowed their cars down to get a glimpse of the King. "He rode his horse near the driveway and entrance to Graceland, looking over the crowd," Pepper said, "And asked the gatekeeper to open the gates and let everyone in.

He sat on his horse and signed autographs and allowed the fans to take photos and ask questions for about two and a half hours. Someone in the crowd asked him about his neck scarf and he took it off and threw it into the crowd. As you can imagine, there was quite a scramble and quite a few fans got a piece of it. Elvis finally got so hot and tired he said he would have to say goodbye to everyone. He continued to do the same thing each day for a week."[3] During the course of that afternoon, it is estimated that between 3,000 and 4,000 people had made their way onto the Graceland grounds to watch Elvis ride.

Safe and secure on the back of his horse, Elvis was able to reconnect with a live audience. It was an experience that would transfer into his performances on stage.

15

THE KING'S LEGACY

By the mid-1970s, a hectic schedule of touring and the pressures of maintaining worldwide fame were beginning to take a toll on the now middle-aged Elvis Presley. Adding to this, he and Priscilla had separated in 1972 and their divorce became final the following year. When Priscilla moved to California, taking young Lisa with her, she also moved her horse Domino to the west coast. For the next four-and-a-half years, Elvis maintained a serious relationship with future actress and songwriter Linda Thompson; however, it is unclear whether the couple ever rode horses together.

During this time, the horses continued to provide comfort to Elvis amidst the many changes in his life. The star was away from home often during his stints in Las Vegas and U.S. tours, but the horses were not far from his mind. When his beloved Tennessee Walker, Bear, passed away while Elvis was on tour, Vernon feared telling him because he knew Elvis would be unquestionably crushed by the loss.

There are very few anecdotes and photographs of Elvis riding horses during the mid-1970s; likely, his performance schedule and a series of health problems kept him out of the saddle for much of the time. However, actress Sheila Ryan, who dated Elvis in the mid-1970s, noted that he bought her a horse that was stabled in the Graceland barn. Additionally, in 1975, Elvis purchased a black Tennessee Walker called Ebony's Double, perhaps to fill the large void left by the death of Bear.

Ebony's Double, foaled in 1972, was a jet-black son of the well-known stallion Ebony Masterpiece. The sire, who had a near hind sock, a star, and a snip adorning his black coat, won the World Grand Championship at the 1962 Tennessee Walking Horse Celebration. Retired to stud the following year, he would sire 3,555 foals during his lifetime, including five sons who also became World Champions.

The flashy Ebony's Double was two years old when Elvis first set eyes on him at the Lennox Farm near Collierville, Tennessee, where he had purchased horses in the past. According to Alene Alexander, who became the Graceland stable manager after Elvis's passing, the King was impressed by the young, coal-colored horse, who was wearing red leg wraps at the Lennox farm. Elvis purchased the horse immediately; later, however, when the gelding was unloaded, sans wraps, from the trailer at Graceland, Elvis was not convinced it was the same horse he had seen. According to Alexander, Elvis requested that the wraps be put back on, at which time he realized that the horse was in fact the one he had purchased. Like Rising Sun, Elvis taught Ebony's Double to drink Pepsi from a can and enjoyed spending time with the tall, smooth-gaited animal.

On a bristling hot mid-August day in 1977, the world was shattered by the news that Elvis Presley, the King, had passed away from a heart attack at his Graceland home. He was only forty-two years old. The world mourned the loss of this man who had singlehandedly touched so many lives. He had affected people from all walks of life, both through his incredible talent and his humanitarian acts, which were done not for show or acclaim, but rather for the pure act of selfless giving. Elvis's body was originally buried near his cherished mother, Gladys, at Forest Hill Cemetery; however, after a failed attempt by grave robbers, the bodies of Elvis and Gladys would be reburied at Grace-land on October 3, 1977.

Elvis's tragic passing not only left behind a slew of grieving family members, friends, and fans, but also a stable of five beloved horses. Following his death, the horses, which included Rising Sun and Ebony's Double, were in need of a new caretaker. When Graceland was opened to the public in 1982, Alene Alexander was hired as a tour guide and quickly noticed that the horses were thinner than they should have been. "Elvis took such good care of them," she explained in the *Mid-South Horse Review*, "but when he died, the heart of Graceland died."[1] Alexander, a lifelong horsewoman, assumed the role of stable manager and quickly restored the horses to good health.

In 1983, Ebony's Double caught the eye of some visitors to Graceland as he grazed in the pasture, his coat shining like black gold. The visitors, who had Tennessee Walking Horses of their own, inquired about the horse and were told that he was a son of Ebony Masterpiece. The visitors suggested to Graceland management that they should consider showing the horse in a special retirement ceremony at the Tennessee Walking Horse World Celebration that fall in Shelbyville, Tennessee. Graceland officials, along with Priscilla, agreed to take part in the ceremony, with Alene Alexander given the honor of riding the horse. It would be a daunting task to ready Ebony's Double for such a lofty appearance, as the gelding had not been ridden since Elvis's

Priscilla Presley poses with Elvis's beloved horse, Rising Sun, at Graceland on
May 4, 1982—nearly five years after the singer's tragic death. *© Ron Galella /
Ron Galella Collection / Getty Images.*

death in 1977. Nevertheless, knowing that the appearance would have made Elvis proud, Alexander agreed to it.

Six weeks later, Alexander rode the beautiful gelding into the ring under the tutelage of trainer Howard Hamilton. Despite the fact that the pair had had little time to prepare for the show, Alexander and her mount rose to the occasion under the spotlights, where all eyes were focused only on them.

"I gave him just a touch," Alexander remembered, "and his head went up and he hit a lick as though he knew just what to do. They brought out a retirement blanket with white silk roses and the outline of a guitar." She added, "The opportunity to show that horse was a turning point in my life."[2]

Many of the horses at Graceland lived long, happy lives, likely as a result of the excellent lifelong care given to them by Elvis, and later by Alene Alexander. Ebony's Double lived to the ripe old age of nearly thirty-two, while Mare Ingram exceeded the life span of most horses, passing away at the incredible age of fifty years. Lisa Marie's pony, Moriah, reached thirty, despite suffering a broken leg many years prior, which was successfully repaired at the Mississippi State University veterinary hospital.

Since Elvis's passing, the Graceland stables have become home to several additional horses. Sun's Reflection, a

Palomino Quarter Horse from the same bloodlines as Rising Sun, and Ebony's Secret Threat (a black Tennessee Walking Horse related to Ebony's Double), carried on the legacy until they passed away. In recent years, the stable welcomed several rescue horses that were in need of homes, reflecting the generosity that Elvis demonstrated throughout his lifetime.

As for Elvis's favorite horse, Rising Sun, the sturdy Palomino outlived his master by nine years, passing away peacefully at Graceland in 1986 at the age of twenty-five. Elvis's beloved equine friend was buried in the far paddock, with his head pointed eternally toward the rising sun. As a tribute to the bond that Elvis shared with Rising Sun, there will always be a Palomino horse living in the stable at Graceland. That, it seems, is just what Elvis would have wanted.

Certain items of Elvis's tack were on display for fans as part of an Elvis-themed exhibit at BreyerFest in 2010 at the Kentucky Horse Park. *Photo © Pablo Alcala/ Lexington Herald-Leader.*

COMING FULL CIRCLE

Decades after his untimely death, Elvis Presley remains one of the most popular icons the world has ever seen. From Memphis to Hollywood, in the United States and abroad, the King's spirit lives on—not only in his music and movies, but also in the world of horses.

In 2010, the Breyer company, which creates world-famous miniature horse sculptures, introduced resin models of both Rising Sun and Bear, celebrating the bond that Elvis shared with his horses. The realistic, limited-edition figurines featured Elvis's signature on the underside of each horse. Breyer also created a line of other Elvis-related horse figurines, along with a set of two holiday ornaments featuring Elvis riding Sun and Bear, as well as a jewelry box, and

This limited edition figurine of Elvis's beloved Rising Sun was released at BreyerFest in 2010. *Photo courtesy of Breyer Animal Creations.*

Breyer's set of holiday ornaments featuring Elvis atop Bear and Rising Sun. *Photo courtesy of Breyer Animal Creations.*

Breyer released this Elvis-themed equine jewelry box as part of its Elvis Collection. The box features photographs of Elvis and a miniature spinning replica of Rising Sun. *Photo courtesy of Breyer Animal Creations.*

a toy replica of the Graceland barn. That summer, the company included an Elvis exhibit at its annual "Breyerfest" celebration at the famed Kentucky Horse Park in Lexington, Kentucky, which featured displays of some of Elvis's tack, photographs, and other horse-related items. The *Lexington Herald Leader* reported on the event, noting that fans were "all shook up" about the Elvis exhibit at Breyerfest, an obvious reference to one of the King's early musical hits.

Elvis also received some recent recognition for his work onscreen in Western films, where he demonstrated his connection with horses. Reel Cowboys, a non-profit Western film and TV appreciation organization, annually presents awards to actors, stunt riders, directors, and other individuals who have worked in Western films or TV series and have served their fellow man through charitable endeavors. In September 2016, Elvis was posthumously presented with two honors from the Reel Cowboys: the Silver Spur Award for his work onscreen in Western films and a medal of honor for his military service. Many Hollywood stars were in attendance at the ceremony, with Jerry Schilling accepting the awards on behalf of his late friend.

Aside from the aforementioned honors, among the most exciting developments to occur in recent years are the plans to restore Elvis's beloved Circle G Ranch. Having changed ownership several times since the 1970s, the property fell into utter disrepair before being purchased in 2014 by a group of investors led by Mississippi native Buddy Runnels Jr. of Real Estate International Inc. Plans are underway to restore the ranch to the original beauty that caught Elvis's eye when he first set foot on the property in early February 1967. The cross that mesmerized Elvis so many years ago will be refurbished and repainted, along with the footbridge he crossed on the back of his trusted companion, Rising Sun. The stables where Elvis spent so much time caring for his beloved horses will also be restored, as will the "honeymoon cottage" where he and Priscilla stayed in the early weeks of their marriage.

Breyer released a limited edition figurine of Elvis's treasured Bear in 2010 as part of the company's Elvis Collection. *Photo courtesy of Breyer Animal Creations.*

Whitney Lee, who, along with Runnels, has been instrumental in the redevelopment of the Circle G, noted, "When we arrived on the property, the first thing I noticed was the cross. It was so much larger than any photo or description could ever convey. The entire property had a sense of peace, serenity and safety…with a touch of mystery from the countless word-of-mouth stories from the friends and family of Elvis, as well as the unique tales that have come throughout the years. No matter what is actually true, I immediately felt like the ranch had a story to tell. Not just about the past, but also in the future."

Once the restoration is complete, plans for the Circle G ranch include the creation of an entertainment destination that will, according to the organization's mission statement, "strive to embrace the local community as well as to ignite an international movement to make a positive impact on aspects that Elvis felt most passionately towards, such as children with special needs, charitable causes, as well as active military and veterans." One such plan includes the development of a riding program that will provide horse therapy to special needs children and adults, as well as to veterans suffering from the traumas of war. The owners of the ranch believe that these causes would be near and dear to Elvis's heart—a heart that was full of love and compassion for others.

As the Circle G property is eventually restored to its former splendor, Elvis fans from all over the world will be able to gain a glimpse into a special time in the star's life when he found the peace and solace that he so desired. Folks will be able to step back in time—to look upon the emerald meadows and fields that Elvis enjoyed exploring on the back of Rising Sun, and to gain a feel for the tranquility that soothed the star's deep and passionate soul. In such a way, at his beloved ranch, the spirit of Elvis will always be alive.

WITH THANKS AND GRATITUDE

The authors wish to thank the following for their contributions to this project:

Larry Geller, for sharing his memories of his friendship with Elvis and their time with the horses at Graceland and at the Circle G; Darlene Tompkins, for sharing her recollections of the filming of *Blue Hawaii*; Russ Howe, for his enthusiastic support, sharing of his vast collection of photographs, and providing us with key contacts and information for this project; Judy Palmer Bendewald, for her memories of Elvis and for allowing us to include her beautiful photographs in the book; Allison Pareis, for her generous assistance with formatting the photographs; Shirley Connell, who shared her memories of Elvis and Rising Sun;

Everett Brown, for sharing his recollections of meeting Elvis and Rising Sun and allowing us to include his song lyrics in the book; Whitney Lee, for providing us with valuable information and photographs of the Circle G Ranch; Our agent, Lyn DelliQuadri, for her steadfast belief in this project, as well as Jane Lahr of Lahr and Partners; Alex Novak of Regnery Publishing for instantly seeing the potential of this unique tribute to Elvis and for his support along the way; Robin Hutton, for her beautiful friendship and kindness of spirit; Patrick Lennon, for his thoughtful review of the manuscript; TanNa Young, for her help and support; and all of our family members and friends for their constant encouragement.

PARTIAL LIST OF HORSES OWNED BY ELVIS PRESLEY

Name	Description
Bear	Elvis's black Tennessee Walking Horse gelding
Beauty	Named after a horse in the James Dean film *Giant*
Big Red	Named for Elvis's friend Red West
Buckshot	Named for Wild Bill Hickok's horse
Colonel Midnight	Vernon's black Tennessee Walker gelding; named for Colonel Tom Parker

Name	Description
Conchita's Gold	A Quarter Horse
Domino	Black Quarter Horse owned by Priscilla
Ebony's Double	Black Tennessee Walking Horse gelding; the last horse Elvis brought to Graceland
Flaming Star	Named for Elvis's film
Golden Sun	A Palomino horse
Guy	A bay horse
Keno	Red West's horse
Lady	No description available
Mare Ingram	A mixed-breed mare named for Mayor William Ingram
Memphis	A Tennessee Walking Horse

Name	Description
Model	A Palomino bought for Alan Fortas
Moriah	Lisa Marie's Shetland pony
Pokey Dunit	Brown Texas-bred horse purchased for Larry Geller
Rising Sun	Elvis' Palomino Quarter Horse gelding
Scout	No description available
Sheba	Sorrel mare bought for Sandy Kawelo
Spurt	A chestnut horse
Star Trek	No description available
Thundercloud	No description available
Traveler	A horse formerly owned by Mary Travers of Peter, Paul, and Mary
Whirlaway	A chestnut horse

RISING SUN

WORDS AND MUSIC
BY EVERETT BROWN

Summertime had final arrived
I was living in Memphis, the King was alive
My car broke down and I was walking to a phone
Past gates of iron and a wall of stone

CHORUS:
I saw the King riding Rising Sun
Early one morning 'cross the Graceland lawn
Shining like a diamond in the delta dawn
I saw the King riding Rising Sun

I never shall forget that face
Clean-shaven every hair in place

Around his throat he wore a purple scarf
His bodyguard behind him in a white golf cart

Rising Sun was the horse's name
A Palomino with a golden mane
A silver saddle and a flashing stride
A pony fit for a king to ride

CHORUS:
I was wishing for a camera along about then
All I had on me was a paper and pen
I held it high as he rod by
That's the way it was for the King and I

The tabloids tell us the King has been seen
In Mississippi playing a slot machine
But I know better that the King is gone
Whatever happened to Rising Sun?

I saw the King riding Rising Sun
Early one morning 'cross the Graceland lawn
Shining like a diamond in the delta dawn
I saw the King riding Rising Sun

Copyright Everett Brown 2003

KEY EVENTS IN THE LIFE OF ELVIS PRESLEY

April 25, 1912: Elvis's mother, Gladys Love Smith, is born in Pontotoc County, Mississippi to Robert and Octavia "Doll" (Mansell) Smith.

April 10, 1916: Elvis's father, Vernon Elvis Presley, is born to Jessie and Minnie May (Hood) Presley in Fulton, Mississippi.

June 17, 1933: Vernon Presley and Gladys Smith are married in Pontotoc County, Mississippi.

January 8, 1935: Gladys Presley gives birth to twin sons, Jessie Garon and Elvis Aaron, at 4:00 AM and 4:35 AM, respectively. Tragically, Jessie Garon is stillborn. (Elvis's middle name was listed as "Aron" on his birth certificate, which Elvis changed to the biblical spelling as an adult.)

January 9, 1935: Jessie Garon Presley is buried at Priceville Cemetery in an unmarked grave.

January 8, 1946: Elvis receives a guitar for his birthday. Legend states that he had wanted either a bicycle or a rifle, but his mother convinced him to choose a guitar instead.

Late 1948: Elvis and his parents relocate to Memphis, Tennessee with their belongings packed in a trunk, which is strapped to the roof of their 1939 Plymouth automobile. They make their home in a public housing project in Memphis.

June 3, 1953: Elvis graduates from L. C. Humes High School. During high school, he works at various jobs to help support his family, including a stint as an usher at a movie theater.

1953: Elvis creates a demo of the songs "My Happiness" and "That's When Your Heartaches Begin" for his mother at The Memphis Recording Service at the Sun Record Company. At the time, Elvis worked as a truck driver.

1954: Elvis releases his first song, "That's All Right," on the Sun label. He and his band begin to perform at various small venues throughout the South.

August 15, 1955: Colonel Tom Parker becomes Elvis's manager.

November 20, 1955: Elvis signs his first contract with RCA Records. He is paid $40,000, with a $5,000 bonus.

January 10, 1956: Elvis records the song "Heartbreak Hotel" at his first session with RCA Records.

January 27, 1956: "Heartbreak Hotel" is released by RCA. The song goes on to sell more than 300,000 copies in its first three weeks. "Heartbreak Hotel" earns Elvis his first gold record award.

January 28, 1956: Elvis makes his first network television appearance on *Stage Show* on the CBS network.

March 1, 1956: Elvis performs a screen test for Hal Wallis and Paramount Studios, which eventually results in his casting in the film *Love Me Tender*.

March 13, 1956: Elvis's first album, *Elvis Presley*, is released.

Summer 1956: Elvis spends time riding horses at the Gulf Hills Dude Ranch with girlfriend June Juanico.

Summer 1956: Elvis makes TV appearances on both *The Milton Berle Show* and *The Steve Allen Show*.

August 1956: Elvis begins shooting *Love Me Tender*, which involves riding and driving horses.

September 9, 1956: Elvis appears for the first time on *The Ed Sullivan Show*.

November 16, 1956: *Love Me Tender* opens at the Paramount Theater in New York City.

January 1957: Elvis begins work on his next film, *Loving You*, in which one scene is filmed in front of a horse paddock.

March 1957: Elvis purchases Graceland for his parents and himself.

May 1957: Elvis begins production on the film *Jailhouse Rock*, in which he stars as ex-con Vince Everett.

December 1957: Elvis receives his draft notice. He requests and is granted an extension in order to film the movie *King Creole*.

January 1958: Elvis begins work on the film *King Creole*. He would receive excellent reviews for his acting in this film.

March 24, 1958: Elvis is inducted into the U.S. Army.

August 14, 1958: Elvis's beloved mother, Gladys, passes away, leaving Elvis devastated.

October 1, 1958: Elvis arrives in Germany for his Army service. He will eventually be promoted to sergeant.

September 1959: Elvis meets his future wife, Priscilla Beaulieu, in Germany.

March 5, 1960: Elvis is officially discharged from active duty.

April 1960: Elvis begins filming *G.I. Blues*.

August 1960: Elvis begins work on *Flaming Star*, which includes a substantial amount of horseback riding.

November 1960: Elvis begins filming *Wild in the Country*.

March 1961: Elvis begins filming *Blue Hawaii*, which includes a scene where he rides a horse on the beach.

July 1961: Elvis begins work on *Follow That Dream*.

October 1961: Elvis reports for filming on *Kid Galahad*.

March 1962: Elvis begins work on *Girls! Girls! Girls!*

August 1962: Elvis begins filming *It Happened at the World's Fair*.

January 1963: Elvis begins work on *Fun in Acapulco*.

July 1963: Elvis starts filming *Viva Las Vega*s, which co-stars Ann-Margret. The two will remain close friends for the remainder of Elvis's life.

October 1963: Elvis begins work on *Kissin' Cousins*.

March 1964: Elvis begins filming *Roustabout*.

July 1964: Elvis begins shooting *Girl Happy*.

October 1964: Elvis starts work on *Tickle Me*, which includes a scene where he sings in a stable of horses.

March 1965: Elvis begins filming *Harum Scarum*, which includes a horseback riding scene.

May 1965: Elvis begins filming *Frankie and Johnny*.

August 1965: Elvis begins work on *Paradise, Hawaiian Style*.

August 27, 1965: Music history is made when the Beatles visit with Elvis at his home in California.

February 1966: Elvis begins work on the film *Spinout*.

June 1966: Elvis begins work on *Double Trouble*.

September 1966: Elvis begins work on his twenty-fourth film, *Easy Come, Easy Go*.

December 1966: Elvis formally proposes marriage to Priscilla.

December 1966: Elvis purchases his first two horses, Domino and Sheba, as gifts for Priscilla and Sandy Kawelo, respectively.

January 1967: Elvis purchases a Golden Palomino Quarter Horse, Midget's Vandy, and promptly renames him Rising Sun.

February 1967: While on a horse-buying trip in Mississippi, Elvis spots Twinkletown Farms, a 163-acre ranch that is offered for sale. He purchases the property and renames it the Circle G Ranch.

March 1967: Elvis begins work on *Clambake*, his twenty-fifth film.

May 1, 1967: Elvis and Priscilla are married in a private ceremony at the Aladdin Hotel in Las Vegas.

June 1967: Elvis begins work on the film *Speedway*.

September 1967: Elvis begins filming the Western-themed comedy *Stay Away, Joe*.

November 1967: Amid pressures from the Colonel and his father Vernon, Elvis agrees to sell the ranch.

February 1, 1968: Elvis's only child, Lisa Marie, is born.

March 1968: Elvis begins work on his twenty-eighth movie, *Live a Little, Love a Little.*

June 1968: Elvis begins work on an NBC TV special that will revitalize his career. The special, entitled *Elvis*, will become known as the *'68 Comeback Special.*

July 1968: Elvis begins work on the western *Charro!*, in which he performs a large amount of horseback riding onscreen.

October 1968: Elvis begins filming his thirtieth movie, *The Trouble with Girls.*

December 3, 1968: Elvis's TV special premieres on NBC and receives rave reviews.

March 1969: Elvis performs his last movie role in the film *Change of Habit.*

July 31, 1969: Elvis begins performing at live concerts in Las Vegas, where he appears to sold-out crowds.

Early 1972: Elvis and Priscilla are separated and will later divorce. Priscilla moves to California with the couple's daughter, Lisa Marie.

July 1972: Elvis begins a four-and-a-half-year relationship with Linda Thompson.

November 1972: A documentary entitled *Elvis on Tour* opens in theaters. The film will later receive a Golden Globe Award for Best Documentary.

April 4, 1973: Elvis's TV special, *Elvis: Aloha from Hawaii via Satellite*, is aired and receives stellar reviews.

October 9, 1973: Elvis and Priscilla are formally divorced.

October–November, 1973: Elvis is hospitalized in Memphis for a variety of health issues.

January–February, 1975: Elvis continues to battle health issues and is hospitalized.

1975: Elvis purchases Ebony's Double, the last horse he brings to Graceland.

November 1976: Elvis and Linda Thompson end their relationship.

Late November 1976: Elvis meets Ginger Alden, the woman who will become his last steady girlfriend.

June 26, 1977: Elvis performs his last concert at Indianapolis' Market Square Arena.

August 16, 1977: Elvis passes away from a heart attack at his Graceland home. He was originally buried next to his mother in Forest Hill Cemetery.

October 3, 1977: After a failed attempt by grave robbers, the bodies of Elvis and Gladys are moved and reburied at Graceland in the Meditation Garden.

June 26, 1979: Elvis's father, Vernon Presley, passes away in Memphis. He is buried in the Meditation Garden at Graceland alongside his wife and son.

1986: Elvis's favorite horse, Rising Sun, passes away and is buried at Graceland facing the rising sun.

Sources: www.elvis.com; Peter Guralnick and Ernst Jorgensen, *Elvis Day by Day: The Definitive Record of His Life and Music* (New York: Ballantine Books, 1995).

THE COMPLETE FILMS OF ELVIS PRESLEY

Year	Film	Character	Horse-Related Scenes
1956	**Love Me Tender**	Clint Reno	Rode and drove horses
1957	**Loving You**	Jimmy Tompkins (Deke Rivers)	Stood in front of paddock with horses in one scene
1957	**Jailhouse Rock**	Vince Everett	
1958	**King Creole**	Danny Fisher	
1960	**G.I. Blues**	Tulsa McLean	
1960	**Flaming Star**	Pacer Burton	Rode horses throughout film; drove a cart

Year	Film	Character	Horse-Related Scenes
1961	Wild in the Country	Glenn Tyler	
1961	Blue Hawaii	Chad Gates	Rode horses in one scene
1962	Follow That Dream	Toby Kwimper	
1962	Kid Galahad	Walter Gulick / Kid Galahad	
1962	Girls! Girls! Girls!	Ross Carpenter	
1963	It Happened at the World's Fair	Mike Edwards	
1963	Fun in Acapulco	Mike Windgren	
1964	Kissin' Cousins	Josh Morgan / Jodie Tatum	
1964	Viva Las Vegas	Lucky Jackson	
1964	Roustabout	Charlie Rogers	
1965	Girl Happy	Rusty Wells	
1965	Tickle Me	Lonnie Beale / Panhandle Kid	Sang in a stable with horses
1965	Harum Scarum	Johnny Tyronne	Rode horses in one scene
1966	Frankie and Johnny	Johnny	

Year	Film	Character	Horse-Related Scenes
1966	Paradise, Hawaiian Style	Rick Richards	
1966	Spinout	Mike McCoy	
1967	Easy Come, Easy Go	Lt. Ted Jackson	
1967	Double Trouble	Guy Lambert	
1967	Clambake	Scott Heyward	
1968	Stay Away, Joe	Joe Lightcloud	Rode grey horse
1968	Speedway	Steve Grayson	
1968	Live a Little, Love a Little	Greg Nolan	
1969	Charro!	Jess Wade	Rode horses throughout film; roped a wild horse
1969	The Trouble with Girls	Walter Hale	
1969	Change of Habit	Dr. John Carpenter	
1970	Elvis: That's the Way It Is	Himself	
1972	Elvis on Tour	Himself	

APPENDIX E

Pedigree of Elvis Presley's Horse Rising Sun

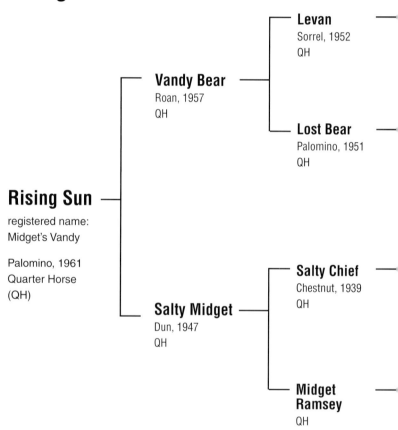

Rising Sun

registered name:
Midget's Vandy

Palomino, 1961
Quarter Horse
(QH)

Vandy Bear
Roan, 1957
QH

Levan
Sorrel, 1952
QH

Lost Bear
Palomino, 1951
QH

Salty Midget
Dun, 1947
QH

Salty Chief
Chestnut, 1939
QH

Midget Ramsey
QH

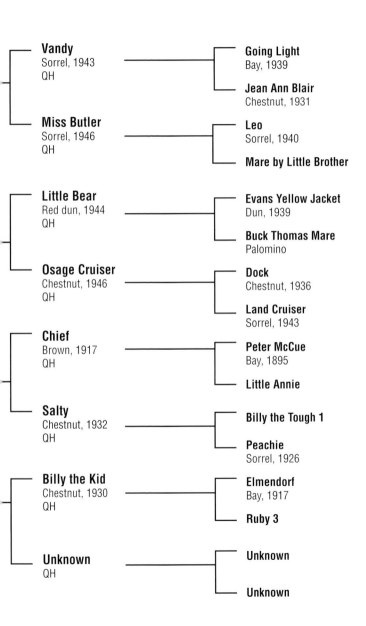

Vandy
Sorrel, 1943
QH

Going Light
Bay, 1939

Jean Ann Blair
Chestnut, 1931

Miss Butler
Sorrel, 1946
QH

Leo
Sorrel, 1940

Mare by Little Brother

Little Bear
Red dun, 1944
QH

Evans Yellow Jacket
Dun, 1939

Buck Thomas Mare
Palomino

Osage Cruiser
Chestnut, 1946
QH

Dock
Chestnut, 1936

Land Cruiser
Sorrel, 1943

Chief
Brown, 1917
QH

Peter McCue
Bay, 1895

Little Annie

Salty
Chestnut, 1932
QH

Billy the Tough 1

Peachie
Sorrel, 1926

Billy the Kid
Chestnut, 1930
QH

Elmendorf
Bay, 1917

Ruby 3

Unknown
QH

Unknown

Unknown

BIBLIOGRAPHY

Bendewald, Judy Palmer. *My Treasured Memories of Elvis*. Memphis Explorations, 2009.

Cantarini, Martha Crawford. *Fall Girl*: *My Life as a Western Stunt Double*. Jefferson, NC: McFarland Publishing, 2010.

Connell, Shirley. *Elvis*: *The Man in My Backyard*. Shirley Connell, 2012.

Curtin, Jim. *Elvis: Unknown Stories Behind the Legend*. Celebrity Books, 1998.

Dietz, John. *My First Tractor*: *Stories of Farmers and Their First Love*. Minneapolis: Voyageur Press, 2011.

Dundy, Elaine. *Elvis and Gladys.* Jackson, MS: University Press of Mississippi, 2004.

Erwin, Sara. *Over The Fence*: *A Neighbor's Memories of Elvis.* Sara Erwin, 1997.

Esposito, Joe. *Good Rockin' Tonight*: *Twenty Years on the Road and On the Town with Elvis.* New York: Simon & Schuster, reissued 2016.

Fortas, Alan and Alanna Nash. E*lvis*: *From Memphis to Hollywood.* London: Aurum Publishing, 1992.

Gaar, Gillian. *Return of the King.* London: Jawbone, 2010.

Geller, Larry. *Leaves of Elvis' Garden*: *The Song of His Soul.* Bell Rock Publishing, 2008.

Geller, Larry. *If I Can Dream*: *Elvis' Own Story.* New York: Simon & Schuster, 1989.

Guralnick, Peter. *Careless Love*: *The Unmaking of Elvis Presley.* New York: Back Bay Books, 2000.

———.*Last Train to Memphis*: *The Rise of Elvis Presley.* New York: Back Bay Books, 1995.

Guralnick, Peter and Ernst Jorgensen. *Elvis Day by Day*: *The Definitive Record of His Life and Music.* New York: Ballantine Books, 1999.

Juanico, June. *Elvis in the Twilight of Memory.* New York: Arcade Publishing, 1997.

Klein, George and Chuck Crisafulli. *Elvis: My Best Man.* New York: Crown Publishing Group, 2010.

Nash, Alanna. *Elvis and The Memphis Mafia.* London: Aurum Publishing, 2005.

Nichopolous, George. *The King and Dr. Nick: What Really Happened to Elvis and Me.* New York: Thomas Nelson, 2010.

Presley, Priscilla Beaulieu. *Elvis and Me.* New York: Putnam, 1985.

Schilling, Jerry. *Me and a Guy Named Elvis: My Lifelong Friendship with Elvis Presley.* New York: Penguin Publishing Group, 2007.

NOTES

Elvis, Elvis Presley, and Graceland are registered trademarks of Elvis Presley Enterprises Inc. (EPE) and Authentic Brands Group (ABG). The text and viewpoints presented in this book are based solely on the authors' independent research and are not in any way affiliated with EPE or ABG.

INTRODUCTION

1. Marco R. della Cava, "All the King's Horses: Graceland Barn Open to Public," *USA Today,* May 28, 2009, http://usatoday30.usatoday.com/life/lifestyle/2009-05-27-graceland-stables_N.htm.

1. A KING RIDES IN

1. Interview with Everett Brown, November 2016.
2. Aaron J. Spicer, "House of the Rising Sun," *The Elvis Mag: Essential Elvis*, Issue 81, (April/May/June 2013).

2. IN THE BEGINNING

1. Interview with Vernon Presley, *Good Housekeeping* (January 1978).
2. Miss Cellania, "Elvis Presley and His Animals," *Neatorama*, June 12, 2011, http://www.neatorama.com/2011/06/12/elvis-presley-and-his-animals/.
3. Ken Sharp, "Shooting the King: An Interview with Elvis Presley Photographer Alfred Wertheimer," *Rockcellar Magazine*, June 8, 2013, http://www.rockcellarmagazine.com/2013/06/08/shooting-the-king-an-interview-with-elvis-presley-photographer-alfred-wertheimer/.
4. Ibid.
5. June Juanico, *Elvis in the Twilight of Memory* (New York: Arcade Publishing, 1997), 71.
6. Joanne Anderson, "Gulf Hills History Reflects an Era Lost in Time (Sampling History)," *GulfLive*, May 13, 2012, http://blog.gulflive.com/mississippi-press-living/2012/05/gulf_hills_history_reflects_an.html.
7. Juanico, *Elvis in the Twilight of Memory*, 100-1.
8. Ibid., 139.
9. Donna Echols, "Elvis in Ocean Springs!" *The Clarion-Ledger*, August 12, 2015, http://www.clarionledger.com/story/life/mslife/2015/08/12/elvis-ocean-springs/31547033/.
10. Anderson, "Gulf Hills History Reflects an Era Lost in Time."
11. Juanico, *Elvis in the Twilight of Memory*, 315.

3. LOVE ME TENDER

1. "Frank Klump—Animal Trainer/Wrangler," Stepping Stone Minature Horses, https://www.stepstoneminis.com/frank-klump

2. Martha Crawford Cantarini, *Fall Girl*: *My Life as a Western Stunt Double* (Jefferson, NC: McFarland Publishing, 2010), 86.

3. Jim Curtin, James J. Curtin, and Renata Ginter, *Elvis*: *Unknown Stories Behind the Legend* (Celebrity Books, 1998), 106.

4. GRACELAND

1. Sara Erwin, *Over The Fence*: *A Neighbor's Memories of Elvis* (Sara Erwin, 1997), 21.

2. Ibid.

3. Ibid.

5. FLAMING STAR

1. Barbara Eden, *Jeannie Out of a Bottle* (New York: Crown Archetype, 2011), 81.

2. Alanna Nash, "Interview with Barbara Eden," *Elvis Australia*, June 6, 2008, http://www.elvis.com.au/presley/barbara-eden-remembers-elvis-presley.shtml.

3. Alanna Nash, *Elvis and the Memphis Mafia* (London: Aurum Publishing, 2005), 187–88.

4. A. H. Weiler, "Review of Flaming Star," *The New York Times*, December 17, 1960.

5. Interview with Darlene Tompkins, December 2016.

6. Ibid.

7. Alanna Nash, "Mary Ann Mobley Remembers Elvis Presley," *Elvis Australia*, February 25, 2016, http://www.elvis.com.au/presley/interview-mary-ann-mobley.shtml.

8. Piers Beagley, "Billy Smith, Elvis' Cousin and Memphis Mafia Member Talks Candidly to EIN," *Elvis Information Network*, January 2006, https://www.elvisinfonet.com/interview_billysmith_part1.html.

6. MY KINGDOM FOR A HORSE

1. Jerry Schilling, *Me and a Guy Named Elvis*: *My Lifelong Friendship with Elvis Presley* (New York: Penguin Publishing, 2007), 161.
2. Ibid.
3. Nash, *Elvis and the Memphis Mafia*, 397.
4. Priscilla Beaulieu Presley, *Elvis and Me* (New York: Putnam, 1985), 219.
5. Nash, *Elvis and the Memphis Mafia*, 397.
6. Gillian Gaar, *Return of the King*: *Elvis Presley's Great Comeback* (London: Jawbone, 2010), 1.
7. Peter Guralnick and Ernst Jorgensen, *Elvis Day by Day*: *The Definitive Record of His Life and Music* (New York: Ballantine Books, 1999), 226.
8. Elizabeth McCall, "All the King's Horses," *Cowboys and Indians* (July 2012).

7. RISING SUN

1. Interview with Shirley Connell, December 2016.
2. Phil Arnold, "Elvis' Fabulous Rings—Part 1," *Elvis Blog*, May 29, 2011, http://www.elvisblog.net/2011/05/29/elvis-fabulous-rings/.
3. Priscilla Beaulieu Presley and Lisa Marie Presley, *Elvis by the Presleys*, directed by Rob Klug (2005, Elvis Presley Enterprises). Cited in Phil Arnold, "Elvis' Circle G Ranch—Part 2," *Elvis Blog*, March 9, 2013, http://www.elvisblog.net/tag/rising-sun/.

8. A NEW BEGINNING

1. Nash, *Elvis and the Memphis Mafia*, 396.

2. John Dietz, "Elvis' Tractor," in *My First Tractor: Stories of Farmers and Their First Love* (Minneapolis: Voyageur Press, 2011), 65.

3. Ibid.

4. Ibid.

5. Alan Fortas, *Elvis: From Memphis to Hollywood* (London: Aurum Publishing, 2008).

6. Interview with Larry Geller, December 2016.

7. George Klein with Chuck Crisafulli, *Elvis: My Best Man* (New York: Crown Publishing Group, 2010).

8. Dietz, "Elvis' Tractor," 64.

9. Nash, *Elvis and the Memphis Mafia*, 396.

9. HOME AT THE CIRCLE G

1. Interview with Larry Geller, December 2016.

2. Phil Arnold, "Elvis' Circle G Ranch—Part 2," *Elvis Blog*, March 9, 2013, http://www.elvisblog.net/2013/03/09/elvis-circle-g-ranch-part-2/.

3. Peter Guralnick, *Careless Love: The Unmaking of Elvis Presley* (New York: Hachette Book Group, 1999).

4. Interview with Larry Geller, December 2016.

5. Klein with Chuck Crisafulli, *Elvis: My Best Man*, 178.

6. Rees Quinn, *Elvis* (CreateSpace Independent Publishing Platform, 2016), 175.

7. Arnold, "Elvis' Circle G Ranch."

8. Klein with Crisafulli, *Elvis: My Best Man*, 176.

10. A PASSION FOR HORSES

1. Klein with Crisafulli, *Elvis: My Best Man*, 178.

2. Interview with Larry Geller, December 2016.

3. Alan Fortas and Alanna Nash, *Elvis: From Memphis to Hollywood* (London: Aurum Press, 2008), 261.

4. Klein with Crisafulli, *Elvis: My Best Man*, 178.

5. Interview with Larry Geller, November 2016.

6. Pat Gallagher, "Priscilla Presley On the Cause She's So Passionate About and the First Time Elvis Took Her Breath Away," *Huffington Post*, March 12, 2014, http://www.huffingtonpost.com/pat-gallagher/priscilla-presley_b_4933783.html.

7. Presley, *Elvis and Me*, 226.

8. Interview with Larry Geller, December 2016.

9. George Nichopoulos, *The King and Dr. Nick: What Really Happened to Elvis and Me* (New York: Thomas Nelson, 2010), 33.

10. Ibid.

11. Ibid.

11. RETURN TO REALITY

1. Jerry Schilling with Chuck Crisafulli, *Me and a Guy Named Elvis* (Waterville: Thorndike Press, 2006), 169.

2. Ashely Elkins, "HED: Jeweler Fit for a King," *Daily Journal*, November 30, 1997, http://djournal.com/news/hed-jeweler-fit-for-a-king/.

3. Nash, *Elvis and the Memphis Mafia*, 653.

4. Facebook post by Priscilla Presley on September 15, 2014, https://www.facebook.com/ms.priscilla.presley/posts/887490794614123.

12. KING OF HEARTS

1. Judy Palmer Bendewald, *My Treasured Memories of Elvis* (Memphis Explorations, 2000).
2. Ibid.
3. Interview with Larry Geller, December 2016.
4. Curtin, *Elvis: Unknown Stories Behind the Legend*, 350.

13. THE MAN CALLED CHARRO

1. Fortas and Nash, *Elvis: From Memphis to Hollywood*, 287.
2. Rita Overhead, "Elvis the Gunslinger," *Elvis Today,* January 12, 2011, http://www.elvistoday.com/index.php/news-clippings 8/3074-elvis-the-gunslinger.html.
3. Ibid.
4. Dennis Schwartz, "Ozus' World Movie Reviews," March 29, 2006.

14. A TRUE PERFORMER

1. Guralnick and Jorgensen, *Elvis Day by Day*, 257.
2. "Photos—Elvis Presley in Concert 1969 + Summer of 1969 at Graceland," ElvisPresleyPhotos.com, http://www. elvispresleymusic.com.au/pictures/1969-elvis-las-vegas.html.
3. Ibid.

15. THE KING'S LEGACY

1. "Elvis Presley: Rising Sun and Other Horses at Graceland," *Elvis Australia*, December 23, 2015, http://www.elvis.com.au/presley/ elvis-presley-rising-sun-and-other-horses-at-graceland.shtml.
2. Ibid.

 **KIMBERLY GATTO** is a professional writer specializing in equestrian titles and sports biographies. She is the author of fifteen books, including the award-winning titles *Belair Stud* and *Sandsablaze*. Kim has written for various equestrian magazines, including *The Chronicle of the Horse*, *Sidelines*, *Equine Journal*, and *Blood Horse*; and her work was featured in the book *Chicken Soup for the Horse Lover's Soul*. A lifelong equestrian and horse owner, Kim competed for many years in local hunter and dressage shows. She is currently the proud owner of Grace, a lovely off-track Thoroughbred, and Flash, a handsome palomino quarter horse cross.

VICTORIA RACIMO is an award-winning filmmaker, producer,

 writer, and actress. She won Best Director for her documentary *One Day* at the 2015 Equus Film Festival in New York City. Victoria has written two animation specials: *A Toucan Can* starring Jason Alexander and *Pirate Jack* starring Alice Cooper. With Alicia Keys, Victoria co-wrote the children's book *Blue Moon*. She was commissioned by the State of Virginia to write and direct *Journey of Destiny* for the 400th anniversary celebration of the landing at Jamestown, which aired on CBS. Victoria was hired to stage two theatrical sequences for Steven Spielberg's film *Lincoln* and was the executive producer on the film *Casi Casi*, which she sold to HBO. Victoria is the founder and president of Palomino Entertainment Group. She is an avid supporter of equine welfare.